AF686598

Turkish Economic Policies and External Dependency

Turkish Economic Policies and External Dependency

By

Hasan Saygın and Murat Çimen

CAMBRIDGE SCHOLARS

PUBLISHING

Turkish Economic Policies and External Dependency,
by Hasan Saygın and Murat Çimen

This book first published 2013

Cambridge Scholars Publishing

12 Back Chapman Street, Newcastle upon Tyne, NE6 2XX, UK

British Library Cataloguing in Publication Data
A catalogue record for this book is available from the British Library

Copyright © 2013 by Hasan Saygın and Murat Çimen

All rights for this book reserved. No part of this book may be reproduced, stored in a retrieval system, or transmitted, in any form or by any means, electronic, mechanical, photocopying, recording or otherwise, without the prior permission of the copyright owner.

ISBN (10): 1-4438-4469-1, ISBN (13): 978-1-4438-4469-7

To the 90th anniversary of the foundation of the Republic of Turkey

TABLE OF CONTENTS

LIST OF TABLES

List of Figures

PREFACE

Since the 1950s, the Turkish economy has been facing crises periodically. Decisions taken after the crisis had not only economic but also social, political and diplomatic consequences.

Total independence was considered the main principle; economic independence was one of the substantial criteria of that main principle, and economic policies were based on it.

In this book, economic independency level at which governments can take independent decisions is defined in terms of macroeconomic variables based on which a model is developed.

The book aims to analyse the economic policies of Turkey from an economic dependency perspective, identify the macroeconomic variables affecting economic dependency, and develop an alternative economic policy considering all of these.

Therefore, for structuring the model to be proposed and define the policies, it is crucial to discuss economic policies particularly in the post-1980 world and their consequences, together with their impacts on Turkey, crises and main variables of the crises, and also compare the economic policies of the Republic period and their consequences as well.

In the book, it is intended to develop an independent economic structure where Turkey can act in her own interests.

CHAPTER ONE

TURKISH ECONOMY: AN INTRODUCTION

From an economic history perspective, human communities have bought and sold goods to each other for a long time, and in this way, various capital accumulation processes and centres were established. In this book, economic dependence is analysed from this perspective, and it is not defined as totally self-enclosed or an internal economic system. In the historical process, it is not perceived as possible. Buying or selling goods to other nations within the economic system (export and import) has not been directly assessed from a dependency perspective, but dependency has been assessed in the perspectives of foreign trade and current accounts, capital movements, industry and energy resources.

From an applied economic policy perspective, Turkey, with the establishment of the Republic in 1923, has followed policies different from its successor, the Ottoman Empire. In the War of Independence, full independence was put forward as the primary condition of living, development and existence with the sixth article of the National Pact, which objected to political, legal, financial, and all limitations that would hinder the development of the country. It was the prevailing view in the first years of the Republic that Ottoman Public Debt Administration, capitulations, privileged foreign capital and foreign borrowing were considered as the main reasons for the loss of the country's financial and political independence. While Ottoman administration was held responsible and foreign borrowing was avoided; and while foreign capital investments were regarded positively with the condition of their compliance to the sovereignty rights of the country, all the privileges requested by foreign capital were rejected (Cosar, 1996a). However, in post-World War II era, Turkey was placed in the West both in political and economic terms, adopted international free trade doctrine, released protective measures, and rearranged foreign exchange rates.

The Republican People's Party abandoned statist policy after the 1947 Party Congress, also foreign borrowing was perceived positively more in this period, and military aid by Truman Doctrine (1947) and economic aid by Marshall Plan (1948) were received (Cosar, 1996b and 1997). After 1950, in order to benefit from the Marshall Plan, a growth policy based on the branches of light industry and agriculture was envisioned and a perspective claiming that planning is not essential was prominent (Cosar, 2005). Although aimed at limiting the role of the state in Turkey, development through increasing public investments and private sector development was targeted, policy based on foreign aid and foreign capital was perceived in the years onwards. Despite some methodological differences, this policy is still relevant. After 1960, the import substitution model, which is also the prevailing perspective in the world, was adopted in order to overcome trade deficit stemming from the economic model based on fixed exchange rate regime and external sources (Ural, 2003, Soyak and Eroglu, 2008). In the import substitution industrialization model, increase in demand for durable consumer goods was met within the country through the contribution of foreign capital, but these manufacturing branches became externally dependent on basic inputs (Yurdakul, 2001). Three main reasons of external dependence in the economy were defined as increase in the weight of industry which was founded externally dependent and called as assembling industry, external dependence in energy due to oil and agriculture being dependent on weather conditions (Yurdakul, 2001). Near the end of the 1970s, the import substitution model blocked by rising prices in energy and growing external debt and trade deficit was abandoned in 1979-1980 with the emergence of neo-liberal policies, called the Washington Consensus comprised of deregulation of the economy via foregrounding market economy, downsizing the state in the economy, and liberalisation of trade and capital movements (Yurdakul, 2001, Mangir, 2009, Ural, 2003). Turkey, adopting neo-liberal policies with the 24th January 1980 decisions, liberalised the trade through free market economy and export substitution model; in 1989, financial liberalisation was also realised through liberalisation of foreign exchange transactions and capital movements with the Decree No 32 on the Protection of The Value of Turkish Currency. From 2000s onwards, the economy is fully integrated with the global economy. Despite the fact that Turkey was ranked as the 17th biggest economy in the world by the end of 2008 in Gross Domestic Product (GDP) figures, trade and current account deficit has become chronic in the country, and economic growth became dependent on external sources after 1980 and particularly due to the economic policies following 1989 (World Bank, 2009, Treasury, 2008a, 2008b, 2008c). Turkish economy, with its outward oriented economic policy and externally dependent industrial structure became dependent on external sources and exporting to the same markets to pay back such sources (debts) (Yurdakul, 2001). Growth based on import and external sources instead of domestic sources or capital accumulation (foreign trade or current account surplus) created the dilemma of growth-balance of payments deficit (Ekzen, 2008). Such a structure led Turkish economy periodically go through economic crisis based on internal causes and also made it susceptible to crisis originated externally. Trade and current account deficit became chronic; however the budget had current account surplus in crisis years (as in 1994 and 2001) (Treasury, 2008a, 2008b, 2008c).

In these periods, achieving growth right after economic shrink coupled with growth in the balance of payments and current account deficit reflects structural problems in the economy. The need for external sources for economic growth appears to be the most significant cause of economic and political crisis. Economic dependency does not only lead to economic consequences, but also influences the decisions on domestic and foreign affairs about the security of the country in international arena. Likely to cause significant problems for the security of the country, such a situation prevents policy design, prioritizing national interests in foreign affairs, military and security issues.

Notwithstanding the aforementioned negative factors, Turkey is located in a geopolitically important place in the 21st century while the need for energy in the world has been increasing. Turkey is located on an alternative route to the Russian Federation in the East-West corridor that is the transit area for the transferring oil and natural gas, which are decreasing energy resources, from the producing to the consuming region. Except for Russian Federation, Turkey is the only country in the region ranked among the top 20 economies of the world (World Bank, 2009). Despite the fact that Turkey is not rich in fossil-based energy resources other than coal, and coal resources requiring special burning techniques due to high sulphur and low calorie, Turkey has a significant industry and economy in the region. Turkey's ability to mobilize the geopolitical potential is subject to the strong economic structure.

However, the current structure of the Turkish economy is dependent on foreign capital for growth, and considering the young population, it poses a problem. It will be hard for Turkey to use geopolitical potential with such an economic structure. Noting all of the aforementioned facts, it is critical to design economic policies changing the externally dependent structure of the Turkish economy. It can be realised only if the main factors of external dependency are defined and policies to eliminate them are designed and implemented.

Within such a framework, this book aims to analyse the economic policies of Turkey from an economic dependency perspective, identify the macroeconomic variables affecting economic dependency, and develop an alternative economic policy considering all of these. Therefore, for structuring the model to be proposed and defining the policies, it is crucial to discuss economic policies, particularly in the post-1980 world and their consequences, together with their impacts on Turkey, crises and main variables of the crises, and also compare the economic policies of the Republic period and their consequences as well.

CHAPTER TWO

ECONOMIC POLICIES IN THE POST-1980 WORLD AND THEIR CONSEQUENCES

1980 was an important year not only for Turkey but also for the whole world, being the year of radical changes in economic mentality. Particularly, state intervention and the development plan model were recommended to the Developing Countries (DC) by the World Bank after World War II for development (Soyak and Eroglu, 2008, Yeldan, 2002). According to this model, recommended in 1980s, it was essential to increase savings and investments in order to solve underdevelopment, it was recommended to implement the development plan based on domestic demand instead of external demand in DC. Requirement to realise several projects for growth and deficiency of domestic savings in DC made foreign financing inevitable. Besides, the dependency approach perceived in the framework of the ECLA-The Economic Commission for Latin America, established under the umbrella of the United Nations in 1948, correlated underdevelopment with the world order and attributed to the external causes and structural dependency. In this perspective, free foreign trade was functioning to the disadvantage of developing countries, and it was recommended to implement an industrialisation policy based on import substitution for peripheral countries with a negative trade balance due to the integration to the free trade system based on comparative advantages and free foreign trade (Soyak and Eroglu, 2008).

Since the 1970s, major falls in the growth rates due to oil crisis and problems in the external debt repayments in DCs, the solution to the depression was identified as capital entering into the investment areas and capital globalisation (Yeldan, 2002).

By 1978, the International Monetary Fund-IMF, the World Bank and the United States of America (USA) reached a consensus on a reform package for Latin American countries, called the Washington Consensus by John Williams in 1990 (Ertuna, 2007, p. 28). Since the beginning of the 1980s, it is observed that the World Bank has changed its policy by the consensus with structural adjustment based on the theory of comparative advantages. This perspective, called neo-liberalism, Bella Balassa, consultant to the World Bank in those years, and Anne Krueger supporting him, emphasized the failure of import substitution policies and argued for the abandonment of protectionism and integration of the world economy, in line with the comparative advantages. The World Bank recommended structural adjustment programs within this framework and cooperated with the IMF (Soyak and Eroglu, 2008).

The series of economic and political decisions, called the Washington Consensus, is a standard market-oriented neo-liberal reform package with 10 articles recommended for the developing or less-developed countries (Soyak and Eroglu, 2008). The main articles of the reform package are listed below (Ozdemir, 2009a, Soyak and Eroglu, 2008):

a. Financial discipline,
b. Public spending for high return and adjusting income distribution (healthcare, education, infrastructure),
c. Tax reform (low rate wide tax base),
d. Set interest rates in the market,
e. Competitive foreign exchange policy,
f. Free foreign trade regime,
g. Liberalisation of foreign capital,
h. Privatisation,
i. Deregulation (eliminating the entry-exit barriers in the markets),
j. Assuring ownership rights.

The precondition of financial aids by the IMF and World Bank after 1980 is the structural adjustment which is a set of free market-oriented economic policies consisting of the above-mentioned ten articles. Structural Adjustment, conditions of the credits given by the IMF and the World Bank within the framework of aforementioned policies is as follows (Soyak and Eroglu, 2008):

a. Liberalisation of imports,
b. Devaluation,
c. Promoting exports,
d. Eliminating or decreasing the support for agricultural sector,
e. Arranging tax system,
f. Decreasing public expenditure,
g. Restructuring, privatisation, closing State Owned Enterprises (SOEs),

h. Liberalising interest rates and reorganising monetary policy instruments.

IMF and World Bank policies were based on neo-liberal ground with the belief that problems in the economy would be solved within a free market framework, it was aimed at downsizing the public sector, liberalisation of the foreign trade and financial markets (financial liberalisation) and opening them for foreign capital, and brief structural transformation through the price mechanism with such policies (Soyak and Eroglu, 2008). It is asserted that an economic atmosphere to periodically pay back at least the interest of the external debts by the DCs and ensuring consistent borrowing phenomenon is targeted (Soyak and Eroglu, 2008).

The most crucial factor of such structure is short-term capital movements (hot money) aiming at benefitting from disequilibrium between the interest and exchange rate. Despite unavailability of a generally accepted definition for hot money, it is known that it has speculative, short term and fluid characteristics, and economic instabilities occur due to such characteristics. The most crucial point of such instabilities is overvaluation of national currency in an excessive foreign currency situation originated from short term foreign capital movements. Hot money movements are headed towards relatively high real interest in national markets resulting in short term foreign currency abundance, and this in return results in overvaluation of the national currency against foreign currencies. In this way, while importing gets cheaper, exporting sectors regress and the current account deficit grows. The economic growth attained under these circumstances is externally dependent and artificial.

Disruption of the critical equilibrium between real interest and foreign exchange rates causes a sudden breakdown in the economy and it does not leave room for central banks to follow an independent monetary interest and exchange rate policy. In an economy completely open to international capital movements without any restriction, interest and exchange rates turn into a single financial factor through combination, and it disenables implementing an independent development strategy consisting of strategic investment and trade targets. Neo-liberal policies and "developing countries" concepts occur in the literature and they are replaced by the "emerging markets" concept. The development model formed within this framework is an outward-oriented structure providing high financial return through tight monetary and financial policies, with lowered devaluation risk. In this structure, the central bank with independent form is only assigned to the duty of protecting the national currency value, and financial policies are directly targeted to the budget with primary surplus. While the borders of public sphere are downsized through cuts in public consumption and investment, all traditional non-profit social infrastructure activities of the public sector become the field of private sector activity (Yeldan, 2002). The above-mentioned economic structural change implementations actually form the stages of the New World Order. The three stages for establishing the New World Order are as follows (Ertuna, 2007, p. 28):

a. First stage, adopting liberal market economy in the world and particularly in underdeveloped and developing countries,
b. Second stage, incorporation of rules and institutions of the capitalist liberal market economy serving for the interests of wealthy countries,
c. Third stage, transformation of economic ideals into political dominance.

Stages do not follow a time sequence, and they can occur in the same time period simultaneously. After 1980, the new economic thinking began to be adopted in the world by World Bank and IMF, and within this framework, free market economy was spread through the requirements of the aforementioned stages in return for financial aid.

Dissolution of the Union of Soviet Socialist Republics (USSR) after 1990, the collapse of socialist economic regime and popular wisdom on the victory of the liberal market economy offered great opportunities for the World Bank and IMF to implement market economy rules, and the main principles of the Washington Consensus, such as liberalisation of foreign trade, liberalisation of capital markets, privatisation and adoption of the principles of the free market to be implemented in former Eastern Bloc countries (Ertuna, 2007, p. 30). One of the crucial steps in these policies is privatisation. In developing countries, SOEs work in strategic manufacturing fields which generally consist of investments in infrastructure sectors, namely transportation, telecommunications or energy. High capital cost requirement of investment in these fields prevents the private sector, particularly in developing countries, from making such strategic investments in these fields. The aim of the privatisation strategy is strategic infrastructure investments and privatisation is the most important instrument used by global companies to dominate infrastructure sectors such as energy, telecommunications and transportation in developing countries. In privatisation of high cost infrastructure investments, global companies have sufficient capital power (Ertuna, 2007, p. 31).

In the second stage, incorporation of rules and institutions was realised by the enactment of the GATT-General Agreement on Tariffs and Trade in 1994 and the World Trade Organisation (WTO) was established for the execution of the agreement. Final negotiations before its signing took 7 years, and in the meetings, known as the Uruguay Rounds, negotiations were located on two main points (Ertuna, 2007, p. 31):

a. Waiving the quotas on the products of textile sector,
b. Restricting agricultural subsidies.

Countries split in half on these issues. Despite the fact that required quotas in textiles was not an implementation hindering foreign trade, while the USA defending liberalisation in trade was against the removal of the quotas, DCs requested the removal in order to sell more textile products. Although the USA adopted completely the opposite attitude in agriculture and asked for the removal of subsidies, Europe and Japan were against that. After all, the main factors in the GATT agreement are as follows (Ertuna, 2007, p. 32):

a. Free movement of goods and services between countries were held; all the barriers in inter-country movements of goods and services were eliminated.
b. A complete agreement was reached in the liberalisation of inter-country capital movements.
c. No decision was reached on free movement of labour.
d. Intellectual property rights were entirely protected. These rights are brand, design, printed circuits, copy rights, local images, etc. and they provide monopolistic advantage to the owners.

Thanks to the GATT, developed countries holding intellectual rights like brands, fashions, designs and information had the opportunity to manufacture their branded products under this protection in any country where it could be manufactured at the lowest cost and they could sell them at any market in the world at the desired price to make the highest profit (Ertuna, 2007, p. 32).

Within the framework of the Washington Consensus, implementing free market economy rules in Asia, Latin America and former Eastern Bloc countries resulted in an inflow of debt and speculative capital, called hot money into the economies of DC, but growing trade deficits and the financing of such deficits through hot money caused crises in Turkey and Mexico in 1994; in Asia, Russia and Brazil in 1997 and 1998 and in

Argentina and again in Turkey in 2001. It is observed that these crises occurred due to the implemented economic policies and free capital movements.

Due to the consequences, one of the most important criticisms on the economic policies proposed by the Washington Consensus is that free markets are not a fundamental element of growth. It is argued that for sustainable growth and long term efficiency, equilibrium between state and market should be ensured, and companies and economies both should be controlled to a certain extent (Stiglitz, 2002, p. 276, 278). Consequences of main justification for the Washington Consensus, sustainable growth and "Stability Assurance, Privatisation and Liberalisation" implemented in 1980 onwards, are analysed in various studies. Results of these analyses are listed in five main topics (Rodrik, 2006):

a. In the economies in transition from socialist to free market economy, unexpectedly large economic collapses occurred and even in a period exceeding 10 years, these economies could not reach their GDP in 1990.
b. Despite significant improvements in major political reforms, political and external effects and continuing aid, no economic development occurred in Sub-Saharan countries and economies became more vulnerable compared to previous years.
c. Due to unforeseeably rapid capital outflow in Latin America, Russia and Turkey, frequent and deep economic crises broke out.
d. Improvement in the first half of the 1990s was short-term and despite abandoning state-based populist and protective regime policies, an increase in GDP per capita in 1990s remained below the average of the period 1950-1980.
e. Argentina, cited as the best practice, encountered a very serious economic crisis in 2001.

As mentioned above, while crises occurred in countries with free market economy implementations in 1990s, however, contrary to expectations, China, India and a few Asian countries experienced just the opposite situation, and with the steady growth, the number of people living under the poverty line decreased both as a percentage and in absolute figures (Rodrik, 2006). These countries implemented policies contrary to the Washington Consensus features (Rodrik, 2006):

a. High level of commercial protectionism,
b. No privatisation,

c. Extensive industrialisation policy implementations,
d. Loose financial and monetary policy implementations.

All of these developments were a source of criticism for the recommended policies. Free market economy is now questioned, despite the fact that complete detachment from the system is not possible, a tendency to the new approaches is observed and it is argued that agreement on Washington Consensus is over (Cavanagh, 2009).

Studies are conducted on the problems faced during implementation to explore the causes. Main factors are listed as attempting to implement the same policies in any environment and disregarding differences; decreasing budget deficit, inflation and custom tariffs; increasing financial liberalisation and privatisation of everything; insistence on fixed targets, disregarding dynamic factors triggering growth due to predictions on efficiency if loss makers are shut down (Rodrik, 2006). In quantitative studies on the countries in and out of transition, it is reflected that structural changes mostly have a lower impact on growth (Olken and Jones, 2005). Also, effort on comprehensive structural reform may result in unrealisable and insistently implemented policy which has negative results. Russia and China are given as examples. It is indicated that the environment in Chinese investments, which is restricted and possible only in partnership with state enterprises, is more successful than the Russian investment environment which is similar to the European one. It is argued that the reason behind this is investors' feelings that investment and profits will be protected more when they cooperate with state enterprises in China, instead of being located in an insufficient and corrupt legal structure in Russia. It shows that the targeted goal (here it is the protection of the investor rights) sometimes should be reached by different means, taking environmental conditions into account (Rodrik, 2006).

Another reason for questioning the Washington Consensus is that the global system and its regulatory bodies (IMF, World Bank, WTO) have the power of sanction on DCs, but not the power to determine and address the accumulated risks in developed countries. Like in 2008, not only people in developed countries but also in DCs had to bear the damage caused by the crisis stemming from financial market regulation deficiencies and public legislation weakness (Sak and Caglar, 2009).

CHAPTER THREE

POST-1980 TURKISH ECONOMIC POLICIES AND THEIR CONSEQUENCES

The oil crisis after 1970 and the embargo after the Cyprus Peace Operation generated a disruption in the balance of Turkish economy. In overcoming the 1980 crisis, significant structural changes were made in addition to the increase in interest rates and devaluation. The planned import substitution system implemented since 1960 was abandoned and transition was made to a neo-liberal economic system, called the Washington Consensus, elaborated in the previous chapter. With the economic measures taken on the 24th of January 1980, Turkey made changes in the economic policy and ensured liberalisation both in trade and capital movements through changes in Law on the Protection of the Value of Turkish Currency by Decree no 32 issued in 1989 (Yurdakul, 2001, Mangir 2009, Oyan 1999). Therefore, post-1980 Turkish economy is analysed in two periods, namely 1980-1989 and after 1989.

Turkish Economic Policies between 1980-1989 and Their Consequences

After 1960, Turkish economy entered a planned period and despite growth in trade balance, growth in borrowings from the USA saved the country from a foreign exchange bottleneck. Import substitution approach was adopted in the period and the demand growth for durable consumer goods was met by domestic manufacturing with the contribution of foreign capital (Yurdakul, 2001). Such manufacturing branches were externally dependent in terms of technology and primary inputs; moreover, lack of competitiveness reduced the foreign market availabilities. Growth in intermediate product manufacturing not parallel to growing investments increased the import, hence external dependency (Boratav, 2009, p. 120). In addition to that, increase in energy prices after the oil crisis in 1970s is a factor in increasing dependency due to excessive external dependency of Turkey in energy (Yurdakul, 2001).

Particularly, increase in oil prices in the 1973 began an increase in prices; national economies in general were confronted with crises. Western Bloc countries maintained exports via credits to DCs, but foreign debt increased due to increasing oil prices, and Turkey depleted foreign exchange reserves in this period and increased the foreign debt (Yurdakul, 2001). The Turkish economy choked at the end of 1970s, and transitioned from an inward-oriented industrialisation structure to an outward-oriented economic policy program after 1980 within the framework of the Washington Consensus explained in previous chapters (Yurdakul, 2001, Soyak and Eroglu, 2008).

IMF stipulated outward-oriented liberal economy policy as a precondition of the loans. It was the main pillar of the Washington Consensus and consisted of conditions such as the liberalisation of foreign trade, devaluation of foreign exchange rates, increasing interest rates, and restricting public spending, monitoring wages and salaries, and incentivising the foreign capital (Yurdakul, 2001). Turkey closed a deal with IMF and implemented stability decisions taken on the 24th of January 1980, abandoned import substitution industrialisation strategy and transitioned to an economic model focused on rapid increase in exports, promoting the cheap-to-produce and foreign exchange earning goods, based on world prices, opened for foreign competition and targeted a reduction in the weight of public sector in the economy (Soyak and Eroglu, 2008).

By Decree No 8/909 issued on the 1st of July 1980, interest rates were liberalised, reserve ratio on deposits were rearranged and a different interest rate implementation was introduced on export loans, and for the purpose of fostering and differentiating the exports, exporter manufacturers were allowed to benefit from customs exemption in input procurement in order to support and differentiate export. By Decree No 8/168 on the Framework of the Foreign Capital Incentives, particularly entrance conditions of foreign banking, was improved, and the stamp duty on imports was lowered from 25% to 1% to liberalise imports (Soyak and Eroglu, 2008). Liberalised interest rate policy increased the interest rates, while freezing the wages restricted the domestic demand and increased the savings. While the decrease in demand caused a fall in the prices of some products, due to the export of some goods, it caused a rise in prices in domestic market (Yurdakul, 2001).

The IMF and World Bank, with a liberal economy program, became determinant actors in the economic policies of Turkey, and prepared a development model with three alternatives for the period 1982-1988 requesting the implementation of a mild growth scenario based on export.

The most important institutional reflection of the liberal economic program on the development plan of Turkey is in 1982 Constitution. In the 1982 Constitution, development planning was taken out from the fundamental duties of the state and economic clauses were reorganised, and the State Planning Organisation (SPO) no longer held the status of constitutional institution. Thus, function and structure of the SPO became vulnerable to politicisation (Soyak and Eroglu, 2008). The 4th Five-Year Development Plan (FYDP), primarily emphasising public sector and industrialisation, was abolished in the first quarter of the 1980s and further development plans of the SPO were concluded according to the structural adjustment policies of the IMF and World Bank. In the Fifth and Sixth FYDPs; the goals were set as privatisation, removing state from the industrial sector to infrastructure investments (Soyak and Eroglu, 2008). In terms of the applicability of the development plans, the following sentence is a clear statement on the subject: "Since Turkish economy is mainly based on an outward oriented competitive market mechanism, one should not expect Development Plans determine the whole economic and social life in detail, and be forceful to realise its predictions" (SPO, 1995, p.21).

The new economic program targeting a liberal economy and envisioning a new trade structure aimed at opening up the domestic market to external competition and liberalising the imports, encouraging the exports and finding new markets outside the country. With the liberalisation of imports, industrial development policy was abandoned and an outward oriented economic policy was adopted after the new program aiming at combating monopolistic prices in the domestic market. Such practice was characterised as surviving with the foreign loans, and at the same time being dependent on exports to the same markets for paying the debts (Yurdakul, 2001). In liberal economic policy, some negative factors emerged as well. Due to overdependence on exports, negations in markets and fluctuations in foreign exchange rates had negative effects on the economy (Yurdakul, 2001).

In the main economic figures of the period (Table 3-1, Table 3-2, Table 3-3, and Table 3-4), it is observed that although the annual average increase in GDP in real terms was 4.8% (1970-1979 5.8%), the economy downsized during 1980, 1983, 1987 and 1988. Although the USD valued 1.7% annually on average in the period, it is observed that starting from 1985 onwards, TL began to value and moreover in 1989, TL valued 11.1%.

It is observed that the inflation, which was 50.8% on average, began to increase after 1986. Besides, after 1980, both exports and imports increased; the current deficit was persistent and reached an average annual value of 1.7 billion USD. As a general characteristic of the Turkish economy, current account deficit turned into surplus due to the downsize in the economy in crisis years, but the effect of crisis in this period was reflected on foreign trade with a one-year lag.

In this period, budget deficits were persistent and the ratio of budget deficit to total revenue was 19.4%. Share of the indirect taxes, namely Value Added Tax (VAT) and Special Consumption Tax (SCT), in total revenue increased and reached 47%.

Table 3-1 Main Macro Economic Figures in Period 1980-1989 (SSI, 2001, Pakdemirli, 2003)

Years	GDP (Million TL-1990 Constant)	GDP (Million USD)	GDP Increase (%-1990 Constant)	USD FX Increase (% Real)	Inflation (CPI %-December)
1980	239	67,457	-5.27	14.4	93.7
1981	284	70,419	18.88	13.9	27.1
1982	298	63,485	5.15	16.6	26.3
1983	288	60,373	-3.33	1.7	37.1
1984	305	58,643	5.68	8.8	49.7
1985	337	66,410	10.6	-2.3	44.2
1986	376	75,018	11.38	-1.4	30.7
1987	354	85,638	-5.65	-17.4	55.1
1988	350	90,495	-1.30	-6.6	75.2
1989	365	106,123	4.23	-11.1	68.8

Table 3-2 Macro Economic Figures Related to Budget in Period 1980-1989 (SSI, 2001, Pakdemirli, 2003)

Years	Budget Deficit (Million USD)	Budget Deficit / Total Budget Revenue	Total Budget Revenue (Million USD)	Total Budget Expenses (Million USD)	Direct Tax / Total Tax	Direct Tax / Total Budget Revenue
1980	-2.154	-18.3	11,762	13.915	62.8	51.6
1981	-1.096	-8.8	12,460	13.556	64.5	54.9
1982	-950	-10.9	8,743	9.693	63.4	57.2
1983	-1.355	-13.6	9,986	11.340	59.4	50.0
1984	-2.610	-34.9	7,478	10.088	58.3	49.3
1985	-1.487	-17.0	8,729	10.216	47.7	39.6
1986	-2.066	-19.7	10,507	12.573	52.0	43.4
1987	-2.978	-24.9	11,971	14.949	49.6	43.0
1988	-2.703	-21.9	12,316	15.019	49.6	40.2
1989	-3.502	-23.9	14,644	18.146	53.4	43.5

Another crucial development is the rapid growth in Turkey's total debt. With an annual average increase of 9.7%, total debt increased from 25 billion USD to 63.4 billion USD. Net capital inflow was 7 billion of 7.4 Billion USD in this period and it was due to the short term capital movements, which were considered as other investments. General movement of the external sources during crisis can also be observed in 1988 and 1989. The share of the private sector's external debt in total external debt increased, related to an increase in the private sector's share in the economy (Table 3-3).

When one looks at the foreign trade figures of Turkey during the new economic program liberalised foreign trade, and an export based system, it is observed that despite an increase in exports, increase in imports increased the trade deficit more. While the trade deficit was 37.3 billion USD in the period 1980-1989, the same figure for the 1970-1979 period was 20.2 billion USD, which means an 85% increase. Current account deficit was approximately the same for both periods, around 10.4 billion USD. Recently, the developing tourism sector relatively met the increasing trade deficit and kept the current account deficit the same. Analysing in terms of macro-economic data, it is observed that targeted or predicted results of the new economic program were not consistent.

Table 3-3 Macro Economic Figures Related to Indebtedness in Period 1980-1989 (SSI, 2001, Pakdemirli, 2003)

Years	Total Debt (Million USD)	Domestic Debt (Million USD)	External Debt (Million USD)	Private / Total External Debt	Total Debt / GDP
1980	25,032	9,298	15,734	8.5	37.1
1981	25,459	8,832	16,627	7.0	36.2
1982	25,972	8,114	17,858	5.1	40.9
1983	32,590	13,776	18,814	8.9	54.0
1984	33,177	12,354	20,823	13.6	56.6
1985	38,854	13,194	25,660	15.6	58.5
1986	47,648	15,442	32,206	17.2	63.5
1987	60,059	19,733	40,326	15.8	70.1
1988	60,651	19,929	40,722	15.0	67.0
1989	63,456	19,576	43,879	15.1	59.8

Table 3-4 Macro Economic Figures Related to Foreign Trade in Period 1980-1989 (SSI, 2001, Pakdemirli, 2003)

Years	Current Account Deficit / GDP	Foreign Trade Deficit / GDP	Foreign Trade Deficit (Million USD)	Current Account Deficit (Million USD)	Import (Million USD)	Export (Million USD)
1980	-5.1	-7.4	-4,999	-3,408	7,909	2,910
1981	-2.7	-6.0	-4,230	-1,936	8,933	4,703
1982	-1.5	-4.9	-3,097	-952	8,843	5,746
1983	-3.2	-5.8	-3,507	-1,923	9,235	5,728
1984	-2.5	-6.2	-3,623	-1,439	10,757	7,134
1985	-1.5	-5.1	-3,385	-1,013	11,343	7,958
1986	-2.0	-4.9	-3,648	-1,465	11,105	7,457
1987	-0.9	-4.6	-3,968	-806	14,158	10,190
1988	1.8	-3.0	-2,673	1,596	14,335	11,662
1989	0.9	-3.9	-4,167	938	15,792	11,625

Table 3-5 Capital Movements (Million USD) in Period 1980-1989 (SSI, 2001, Pakdemirli, 2003)

Years	Capital Movements	Foreign Direct Investment	Portfolio Investment	Other Investment	Reserve Assets
1980	1,974	18	0	2,450	-494
1981	1,287	95	0	1,387	-195
1982	1,027	55	0	1,260	-288
1983	1,514	46	0	1,536	-68
1984	970	113	0	920	-63
1985	1,850	99	0	1,391	360
1986	1,583	125	146	1,475	-163
1987	1,312	106	282	1,060	-136
1988	-2,111	354	1,178	-2,922	-721
1989	-1,932	663	1,386	-1,509	-2,472

Turkish Economic Policies between 1989-2008 and Their Consequences

By Decree No 32 on the Protection the Value of Turkish Currency issued in 1989, foreign exchange transactions and capital movements were liberalised. Trade liberalisation and full integration with the free market based economic system was ensured in the financial area with the 24th January Decisions. Export was supported by lower value of TL against foreign currencies; but it caused valuation of TL due to the exchange rates lower than inflation after liberalisation of the exchange rates. This policy provided the conditions for the flow of hot money to Turkey (Yurdakul, 2001). In order to decrease the foreign trade deficit in the country, the need for foreign sources emerged and it was met by capital borrowing and hot money from abroad (short term capital movements). The program based on external sources caused high interest rates in TL and low exchange rates, and since a significant portion of the external sources coming to Turkey was hot money, this resulted in a "High Interest Rates, Low Foreign Exchange Rate" cycle (Ertuna, 2007, p. 52, 53, 105). In these circumstances, hot money (foreign currency) entering for high interest rates causes a fall in the exchange rates and leads to an increase in exchange based revenue, and this in turn leads to the flow of more hot money into the country, called a vicious cycle. Low rates on the one hand make imports cheaper, on the other hand complicate exports and cause a growth in current account deficit. Requirement for foreign borrowing caused by current account deficit reaching insecure levels led to the outflow of the hot money, and that causes crises, as in the cases of 1994 and 2001.

Turkish economy, having a structure to grow with external demand and external sources, cannot engage in production when it cannot import or access finance, and then downsizes (Ekzen, 2008). As observed in the growth in the post-1980 economy, import, trade deficit and current account deficit grow increasingly in growth years, but in economic crisis years, current account deficit turns into a surplus and trade deficit decreases. One exception to that is the 2009 crisis. Current account deficit decreased but did not turn into a current account surplus due to a downsizing in the economy. The most important reason is that industrial sector was based on foreign borrowings of 74% and dependent on imports (Ekzen, 2008).

In this period, another implementation, especially after the 2000s, is privatisation. One of the main reasons behind privatisation, which is one of the main pillars of the Washington Consensus, is the fact that public enterprises have ineffective operations due to political interventions and monopolistic status (Ertuna, 2007, p. 121). It was emphasised that the objective of privatisation was to make these institutions operate efficiently. Notwithstanding this, in academic studies it is observed that the actual reason for the increase in efficiency is not privatisation but increasing competition. Also, it is assessed that public monopolies are better than private sector monopolies (Ertuna, 2007, p. 121). While privatisation in Turkey until the 2000s was concentrated on loss-making institutions, after the 2000s, it became a goal instead of a tool to achieve the aforementioned goals, profitable and monopolistic enterprises were privatised and privatisations to generate budget revenues, which are not listed among the targets, were made (Ertuna, 2007, p. 122).

Table 3-6 Main Macro Economic Figures in Period 1990-2008 (TurkStat, 2008a, CBRT, 2009a, 2009d)

Years	GDP (Million TL-1990 Constant)	GDP (Million USD)	GDP Increase (%-1990 Constant)	USD FX Increase (% Real)	Inflation (CPI %-December)
1990	393	150,833	7.80	-24.2	60.4
1991	368	151,262	-6.33	-6.6	71.1
1992	385	159,321	4.55	-0.7	66.0
1993	408	180,652	5.95	-6.6	71.1
1994	353	130,315	-13.44	20.0	125.5
1995	396	169,905	12.16	-14.0	78.9
1996	419	177,882	5.84	1.1	79.8
1997	411	185,435	-1.96	-5.9	99.1
1998	439	197,685	6.72	0.1	69.7
1999	385	181,462	-12.18	-4.3	68.8
2000	446	198,020	15.78	6.1	39.0
2001	379	142,843	-15.01	17.8	68.5
2002	455	183,079	19.95	-6.4	29.7
2003	498	241,126	9.47	-16.9	18.4
2004	545	302,940	9.43	-12.9	9.4
2005	572	363,599	5.06	-12.5	7.7
2006	617	401,457	7.88	-2.3	9.7
2007	633	494,906	2.57	-16.8	8.4
2008	648	553,356	2.38	-8.4	10.1

In the analysis of the progress in macro-economic figures in this period, annual average GDP growth was 3.5%. Despite this, in the 1991, 1998 and 2001 crises, the economy downsized and it repeated in 1999 due to the Asia crisis. The impact of the world crisis in 2008 is observed in 2009 and the economy downsized by 5.8%. Although TL valued annually at 4.9% on average in 2009, annual valuation of TL was 10.2% on average in the period 2002-2008, especially after the 2001 crisis.

In the same period, while average inflation was 52.5%, rapidly decreasing inflation with the help of the inflation target following the 2001 crisis and cheap foreign currency, reached 10.1% at the end of year 2008. Hot money increased the supply of foreign exchange in the domestic market, made foreign exchange cheaper, and cheapening imports significantly contributed to the fall of inflation.

Table 3-7 Macro Economic Figures Related to Budget in Period 1990-2008 (Treasury, 2008a, 2008e)

Years	Budget Deficit (Million USD)	Budget Deficit / Total Budget Revenue	Total Budget Revenue (Million USD)	Total Budget Expenses (Million USD)	Direct Tax / Total Tax	Direct Tax / Total Budget Revenue
1990	-5.099	-24.1	21,197	26,297	52,1	42,8
1991	-8.046	-34.6	23,224	31,270	52,3	42,5
1992	-6.912	-27.2	25,387	32,299	50,4	41,0
1993	-12.201	-38.1	32,030	44,232	48,6	36,5
1994	-5.126	-20.4	25,101	30,227	48,3	38,1
1995	-6.930	-22.7	30,512	37,443	42,5	33,0
1996	-14.909	-45.8	32,537	47,447	39,4	32,7
1997	-14.409	-39.0	36,977	51,386	40,7	33,6
1998	-13.997	-31.1	44,997	58,995	46,6	36,2
1999	-21.200	-47.7	44,474	65,674	45,3	35,4
2000	-20.418	-38.1	53,654	74,073	40,9	32,1
2001	-22.871	-55.1	41,483	64,354	40,4	31,0
2002	-25.779	-51.2	50,391	76,171	33,7	26,3
2003	-26.686	-39.7	67,183	93,869	33,0	27,7
2004	-21.321	-27.4	77,911	99,233	31,1	25,3
2005	-7.271	-7.1	102,975	110,246	30,6	23,7
2006	-3.234	-2.7	120,846	124,080	31,5	24,9
2007	-11.161	-7.6	146,457	157,618	33,9	27,3
2008	-13.360	-8.3	160,640	174,000	35,1	28,2

In analysing the budget figures in the same period, it is observed that while the ratio of the budget deficit to total revenues was 30% on average, the same figure for the post-2001 period happened to be 20%. Showing a fall tendency, budget deficit was 8.3% as of 2008, but increased again and reached 24.3% in 2009 due to the crisis. Decreasing budget deficit due to financial discipline and privatisations did not turn positive and public debt stock continued to increase rapidly in the same period.

Table 3-8 Macro Economic Figures Related to Indebtedness in Period 1990-2008 (Treasury, 2008a, 2008c, 2008d, 2008f, TurkStat, 2008a)

Years	Total Debt (Million USD)	Domestic Debt (Million USD)	External Debt (Million USD)	Private / Total External Debt	Total Debt / GDP
1990	74,320	21,942	52,377	20.6	49.3
1991	77,064	23,441	53,623	20.8	50.9
1992	86,899	28,303	58,595	26.3	54.5
1993	103,085	32,573	70,512	33.4	57.1
1994	95,631	26,926	68,705	25.0	73.4
1995	105,737	29,790	75,948	28.7	62.2
1996	117,218	37,919	79,299	33.7	65.9
1997	124,762	40,407	84,356	39.7	67.3
1998	140,309	43,958	96,351	43.6	71.0
1999	156,848	53,725	103,123	46.6	86.4
2000	176,491	57,889	118,602	45.9	89.1
2001	211,395	97,803	113,592	37.1	148.0
2002	228,373	98,850	129,523	33.2	124.7
2003	274,377	130,285	144,092	33.9	113.8
2004	318,942	157,963	160,979	39.7	105.3
2005	352,393	182,681	169,712	49.4	96.9
2006	382,764	175,170	207,593	58.0	95.3
2007	446,622	197,196	249,426	64.2	90.2
2008	488,934	210,632	278,302	66.8	88.4

The 144 billion USD total public debts at the end of year 2001 reached 288 billion USD at the end of year 2008. Turkey's total debt reached 489 billion USD. An increasing of debt stock despite the revenues gained from the privatisation of profit making SOEs, which generally have the status of monopolies, increases the probability of encountering more chronic budget and current account deficits in coming years.

Being destitute of SOE profits after privatisation would lead to increasing budget deficits, profit transfer of SOEs and increasing imports as a result of their new managements, and more externally dependent manufacturing management would lead to increasing trade and current account deficits. The first indicators appeared in 2009 and current account deficit, which generally turns positive in crisis periods in the downsizing of the economy, could not turn positive for the first time in 2009 even when the economy downsized due to the crisis by 5.9%, which was 14 billion USD.

When analysis is based on total debts of Turkey, in this period, borrowing continued increasingly, the annual average increase rate was 10.4%, the total of internal and external debts reached 489 billion USD and external debt reached 289 billion USD at the end of year 2008. Another important point is that Private Sector External Debt/Total External Debt ratio which had been 20.6% in 1990 and 33.2% in 2002 reached 66.8% in 2008 (Figure 3-1).

Figure 3-1 Total Debt of Turkey in Period 1990-2008 (Treasury, 2008c, 2008d, 2008f)

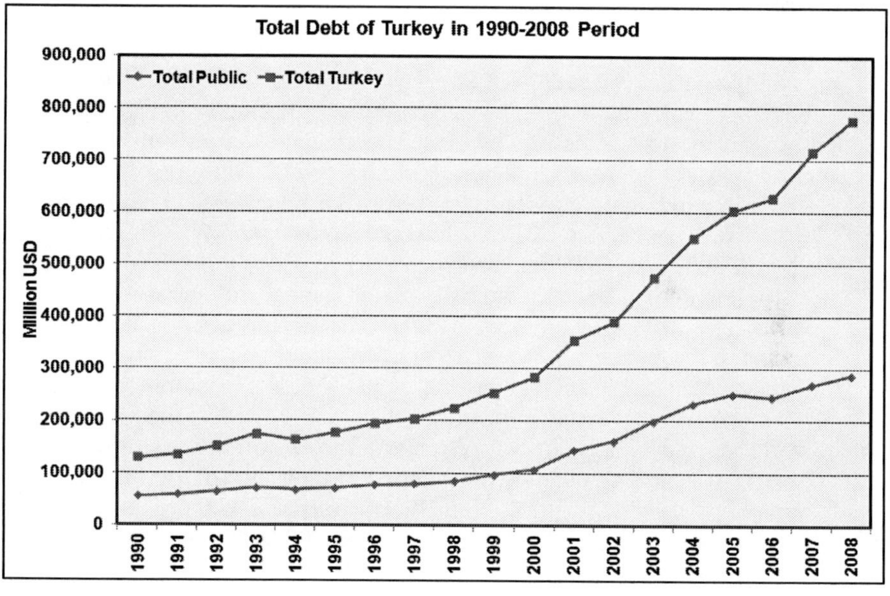

Another reason for the increase in the share of the external debt of the private sector, which is one of the most important instruments to finance the trade and current deficits, is the negative costs stemming from borrowing in foreign currency. The fact that borrowing in foreign currency was cheaper than borrowing in TL (lower interest rates) and USD (reference currency unit in terms of foreign currency in Turkey) was annually devalued 10.1% in the period 2002-2008, created an opportunity for private sector companies not to pay interest in real terms for the USD type loans and even gain an interest income.

In terms of public sector, it is observed that public external debt remained at a level of 70 billion USD and domestic debt at a level of 98 billion USD in 2001, increasing to 210 billion USD by the end of 2008. In this period, the average interest rate for current domestic debt was around 22%; public sector's preference for low cost domestic borrowing instead of borrowing in foreign currency generated a profit opportunity through arbitrage for the ones who were able to access external sources. The ratio of total debts to GDP reached 38% as of 2008. The average of the rate, which was 24.6% for the 1990-2001 periods and, except for the 2001 crisis, had never reached the 30% level, was 47.6% for the period 2002-2008 and never dropped below 30%.

Although the annual average current deficit after 1989 was 9.1 billion USD, the same thing happened in current account deficit, like in other macro-economic developments. While the average deficit was 1.6 billion USD between 1990 and 2001, the current account deficit increased rapidly after 2001 and it reached 22.4 billion USD between 2002 and 2008 and 41.8 billion USD as of 2008. The same progress occurred in foreign trade, too and despite the increase in exports, imports increased as well and the ratio of the trade deficit to GDP reached 12.6% as of 2008.

In this period, annual capital inflow was 8.6 billion USD on average, while it was 1.8 billion USD on average in the period 1990-2001, it reached 20.3 billion USD on average annually in period 2002-2008. In the post 2001 period, a large amount of foreign capital inflow is observed. These figures also confirm that capital inflows are significant in the financing of the increasing current account deficit.

When one looks at the sources of capital inflows, it is observed that 63% is short term capital movements, called hot money and portfolio investments, and 37% is direct investments. The rate of direct investments flowing into Turkey through privatisations and acquisitions rose from 22% in the period 1990-2001 to 37% in the period 2002-2008. The annual average direct investment figure for the period 2002-2008 was 9.7 billion USD; approximately 42%, corresponding to 4.1 billion USD, was from privatisations (Figure 3-2).

Table 3-9 Macro Economic Figures Related to Foreign Trade in Period 1990-2008 (Treasury, 2008b, TurkStat, 2008a, 2008b)

Years	Current Account Deficit/ GDP	Foreign Trade Deficit/ GDP	Foreign Trade Deficit (Million USD)	Current Account Deficit (Million USD)	Import (Million USD)	Export (Million USD)
1990	-1.7	-6.2	-9,343	-2,625	22,302	12,959
1991	0.2	-4.9	-7,454	250	21,047	13,593
1992	-0.6	-5.1	-8,156	-974	22,871	14,715
1993	-3.6	-7.8	-14,083	-6,433	29,428	15,345
1994	2.0	-4.0	-5,164	2,631	23,270	18,106
1995	-1.4	-8.3	-14,072	-2,339	35,709	21,637
1996	-1.4	-11.5	-20,402	-2,437	43,627	23,224
1997	-1.4	-12.0	-22,298	-2,638	48,559	26,261
1998	1.0	-9.6	-18,947	2,000	45,921	26,974
1999	-0.5	-7.8	-14,084	-925	40,671	26,587
2000	-5.0	-13.5	-26,728	-9,920	54,503	27,775
2001	2.6	-7.0	-10,065	3,760	41,399	31,334
2002	-0.3	-8.5	-15,495	-626	51,554	36,059
2003	-3.1	-9.2	-22,087	-7,515	69,340	47,253
2004	-4.8	-11.3	-34,373	-14,431	97,540	63,167
2005	-6.1	-11.9	-43,298	-22,088	116,774	73,476
2006	-8.0	-13.5	-54,041	-32,051	139,576	85,535
2007	-7.7	-12.7	-62,791	-38,219	170,063	107,272
2008	-7.6	-12.6	-69,936	-41,866	201,964	132,027

It is observed from the data that Turkey also used foreign borrowing, in addition to capital movements like privatisation and company acquisitions in the financing of the current account deficit in this period. Another crucial factor is that, particularly after 2001, TL valued and foreign currency based revenues increased and it was the driving force behind foreign borrowing. In the period 2002-2008, the USD based annual real average return of Treasury Bills (T-Bills) was at a high level around 22%. Considering the fact that this return was negative before 2001 and returns were low due to excess liquidity in the world after 2001, the reason for the increase in external debt and capital movements towards Turkey could be understood better.

Figure 3-2 Privatisation Revenue in Period 1990-2008 (CBRT, 2009b)

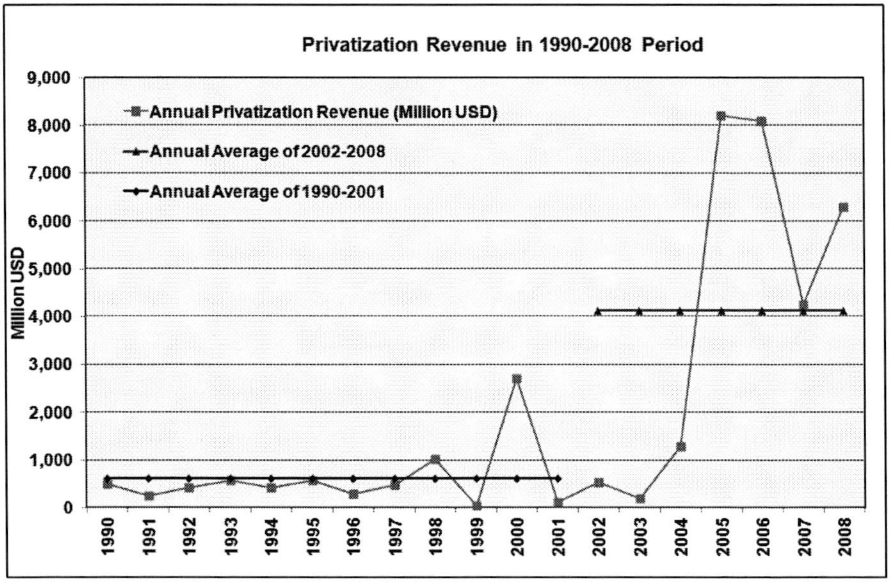

After the liberalisation of capital movements and ensuring financial liberty in 1989, Turkey integrated with the world in terms of commercial goods and capital movements; however it faced many crises. Changes in the world economy in the 2000s and the emergence of China as an important player and the manufacturing centre of the world have changed the balance. In analysing the progress in the data, it is observed that the year 2001 was a breaking point. In Turkey, which integrated with world markets by the implemented policies after the 2001 crisis, privatisation has become an important policy; although economic growth has been achieved, the cost of the growth is increased external debt, current account deficits, and high unemployment rates. Despite positive results in inflation and budget, due to no changes in the budget structure (revenues were heavily dependent on indirect taxes and one-shot revenues like privatisation had an important share), a structure occurred resulting in a decrease in the tax revenues based on imports and consumption taxes with a decrease in imports and consumption. The best example of this is the year 2009 when the budget deficit rose to 24% due to a decrease in imports and consumption after crisis. High unemployment rates occurred despite high growth, reflecting that growth is based on an increase in efficiency. Moreover, it is discovered that privatisations have an important role in increasing unemployment and that they cause problems in the increase of income stemming from the growth. Consumption by individuals could only be possible through borrowing in this period, equilibrium in budget and growth could be possible by increasing borrowing due to increasing disequilibrium in the distribution of income. While average annual domestic loans per capita was 626 USD between 1990-2001, the same figure increased to 1560 USD for the period 2002-2008 and it reached 3192 USD by the end of 2008 (Figure 3-3).

Figure 3-3 Domestic Loan Per Capita in Period 1990-2008 (CBRT, 2009c)

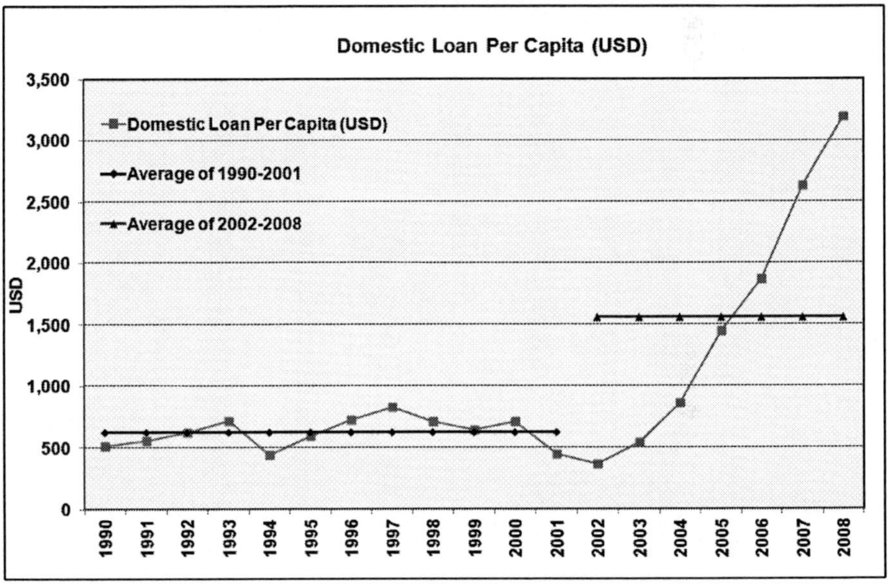

Turkey, having transitioned to a free market economy by 1980 decisions, has moved to an import and free market based economic model to overcome capital accumulation and foreign currency bottleneck and by lifting the restrictions in imports and establishing financial liberty, it has integrated with the world financial system. Although the most important reason for the economic model change was to obtain the capital accumulation required for economic growth from exports, the results reflect a contrary situation. When one looks at the foreign trade figures of Japan, Germany and China, which are export based economies, such difference is observed (Figure 3-4). While Turkey has been giving increasing deficits in foreign trade, trade surplus is observed in these countries.

Table 3-10 Capital Movements (Million USD) in Period 1990-2008 (Treasury, 2008b)

Years	Capital Movements	Foreign Direct Investment	Portfolio Investment	Other Investment	Reserve Assets
1990	3.093	700	547	2.742	-896
1991	-1.198	783	623	-3.803	1.199
1992	2.164	779	2.411	458	-1.484
1993	8.595	622	3.917	4.364	-308
1994	-4.463	559	1.158	-5.634	-546
1995	-93	772	237	3.903	-5.005
1996	938	612	570	4.301	-4.545
1997	3.625	554	1.634	4.753	-3.316
1998	-1.287	573	-6.711	5.067	-216
1999	-377	138	3.429	1.782	-5.726
2000	12.581	112	1.022	11.801	-354
2001	-1.633	2.855	-4.515	-2.667	2.694
2002	1.384	939	-593	7.191	-6.153
2003	3.065	1.222	2.465	3.425	-4.047
2004	13.360	2.005	8.023	4.156	-824
2005	19.460	8.967	13.437	14.903	-17.847
2006	32.064	19.261	7.373	11.544	-6.114
2007	36.622	19.940	717	23.997	-8.032
2008	36.357	15.750	-5.046	24.596	1.057

Turkish economy, particularly with the policies implemented after 2001, has grown through imports and consumption; in order to maintain imports and finance current account deficit, Turkey has resorted to borrowing with high interest rates and selling its assets, and in order to maintain consumption, it has resorted to increasing per capita indebtedness. Turkey, in the excessive liquidity around the world after the 2000s, has become a good source of returns for the capital whose returns were decreasing.

Figure 3-4 Foreign Trade Surplus of China, Japan and Germany in Period 1995-2008 (UFT, 2008a, 2008b, 2010a, 2010b)

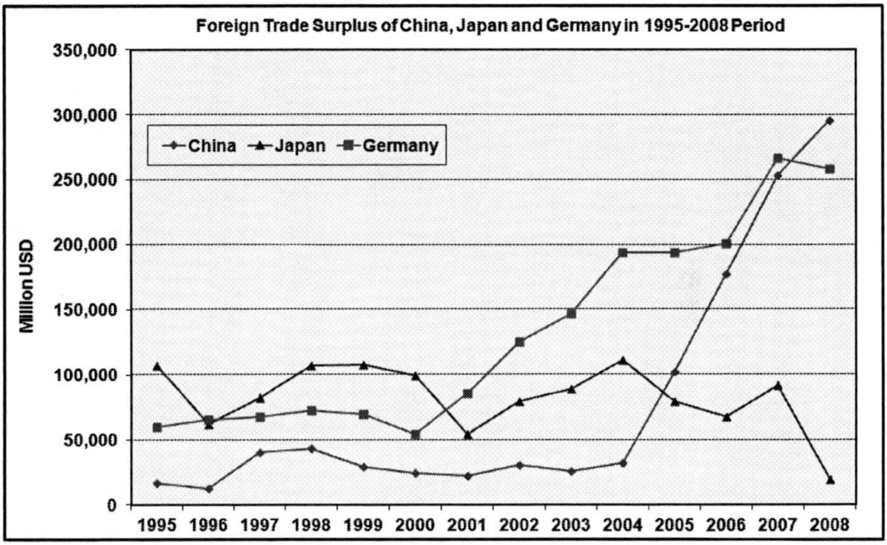

CHAPTER FOUR

POST-1980 CRISES OF THE TURKISH ECONOMY AND MAIN VARIABLES OF THE CRISES

Turkey, which issued trade freedom in 1980 and fiscal freedom in 1989, could not escape from crises despite economic policy change implemented to prevent crises. As is the case all around the world, crises were experienced in Turkey after financial liberalisation (Ural, 2003). Although the capital movements increased, after fiscal freedom was achieved, without macro-economic stability or adequate legal and institutional arrangements affected growth positively, they also increased financial vulnerability and lead to financial instability, and crises occur due to an unsustainable situation (Ural, 2003, Mangir, 2009). As a result of crises, economic and social policies requested by IMF and World Bank had to be implemented in a way that restricted the economic and political independence of Turkey. Since the 1980s, it has been an important reality that in the crisis environment, in return for providing the necessary funds to recollect its economy, the Western world has made Turkey accept the policies which would not be accepted in normal conditions. Some of the policies are economic in purpose and in the name of globalisation; they eliminate the economic growth process as well as economic independence. Some of the policies however are political in character and they increase the financial deficit of the country and due to these policies applied against its own will, Turkey can face negative consequences in its relations with other nations (Kazgan, 2009). While crises can arise from internal factors, they can also arise from external factors. As the integration degree of the economy with the external world increases or dependency increases, the government's ability for market intervention and effectiveness of the interventions decreases. It is normal that crises experienced in Turkey in the 1990s with peaked outward-openness due to external impositions and institutional relations and strengthening of destabilizing factors, reflected from the world occurred simultaneously (Kazgan, 2009).

In addition to the economic consequences, crises also have important political consequences. These are impositions of policy implementations which are not possible to implement in the usual course of events. For example, the 24th of January 1980 decisions could be implemented in the extraordinary conditions of the coup d'état, dated 12 September 1980, and Turkish economic policies were under the control of IMF and World Bank and did not coincide with Turkish interests.

In her study in 2001, Gulten Kazgan states that (Kazgan, 2009) the policies requested by the IMF and World Bank to implement under the name of the program for economic strengthening will eliminate the economic structure and agriculture sector in the first place; that when the implementation of this program is completed, Turkey will have to import many of the products that it has been exporting; that the manufacturing and service sectors will largely switch into the hands of international monopolies; and that the economic structure removed by the Republic will have returned. In the course of time, when this study was conducted, it is observed that almost all of these developments occurred.

In analysing from a perspective of crisis and political consequences, examples of the concessions provided by Turkey after the 1978 crisis included waiving its veto without receiving concessions, and approving Greece's return to NATO's military wing. Following the 1998 crisis (when a stand-by agreement was signed in December 1999), the acceptance of international arbitration by changing the constitution and degrading the Council of State to the level of an advisory board and having to implement the GATT's agriculture policies (leaving the concessions provided to developing countries aside) in a most advanced way (sugar, tobacco laws) are examples of concessions provided. It is stated that a country whose economy has weakened, economic structure is dependent on external sources and must secure sources from international markets within the framework of the IMF, World Bank or free market conditions, will not have much power to object to the demands of the USA (Kazgan, 2009).

As mentioned at the beginning of this chapter, the commercial and financial liberalisation policies of Turkey after 1980 do not prevent crises; on the contrary, due to the fact that they facilitate further integration with the world and increase financial vulnerability, they turned into a form that produced more crises.

Since economic crises in Turkey play a crucial role in political decision making mechanisms and in policy making, it is necessary for Turkey not to experience crisis, or in a more appropriate statement, it should not be in an economic environment leading towards crisis (Kazgan, 2009). Therefore, the reasons for crises and indicators of crises should be identified and preventive policies should be designed.

In general, crisis is defined as having the negative effect of disruptions emerging in financial markets on the performances of financial institutions and as a result of their spread to the whole economy, the deterioration of payment systems and preventions in effective distribution of resources (Isik, Duman and Korkmaz, 2004). Generally speaking, there are four types of crises (Cinko, 2008, Yay, 2001): Monetary crisis, banking crisis, systemic financial crisis, and external debt crisis.

Monetary crisis is as a sudden movement in the FX rate and a sharp change in capital flows causing devaluation of the currency or a large amount of reductions in foreign currency reserves to prevent the devaluation of the currency or astronomic increases in interest rates. Monetary crisis is simply explained as a significant devaluation of the currency (Isik et al., 2004, Yay, 2001). Banking crisis however emerges when the unsuccessful management of banks prevents banks from fulfilling their obligations or when the government is forced to intervene to prevent this failure (Isik et al., 2004, Yay, 2001). Systemic financial crises are defined as the financial disorders which hinder the effective functioning of financial markets and which have negative effects on the real economy. External Debt crisis on the other hand emerges when a country cannot pay back its external debt (Isik et al., 2004, Yay, 2001). A common characteristic of all financial crises is that they have an unsustainable economic disequilibrium and significant fluctuations in financial asset prices (or in FX rates). When the reasons for the crises in the 1990s are analysed, it is observed that macro-economic factors (unsustainable disequilibrium) and financial liberalisation (capital movements or foreign exchange rate systems) are distinguished (Yay, 2001, Eren and Suslu, 2001).

When the economies are analysed from the perspective of unsustainable macro-economic structure, it is observed that, starting from the 1990s, growth in DCs are based on external sources, namely capital movements. This economic model wipes out the chances to implement monetary or financial policy independently. In the case of liberal capital mobility, since countries can control interest rates or FX rates, it is impossible to implement fully independent economic policies. By putting the foreign currency rates under control, DCs have been implementing a free interest rate and hot money policy. In fixed foreign exchange rate policy, persuasiveness of the targeted rate is under the influence of political mistakes and instability, production shocks, weakness of the financial sector and increase in debts (Eren and Suslu, 2001). Excessive short term borrowing increases asset prices as detached from the real economy, financial accumulation causes separation from the real economy over time and it causes weakness in the financial sector by drawing away from self-sustainability. Due to the fixed FX rate, short term foreign capital flows increase real FX rate in the extreme, and this in turn leads to a change in the direction of the hot money, namely leaving country and thus, economic crisis.

One of the most fundamental reasons for the financial crises experienced in the 1990s is the unlimited liberalisation in capital movements. The globalisation efforts intensifying since the 1990s caused a change in the traditional (direct investment) functions of capital movements. Capital movements which take up a short term structure lead to extreme variability in the economies. Without maintaining necessary macro-economic conditions (balanced budget, price stability, fair income distribution, manufacturing of high value added goods, an audited banking system, a financial sector with depth, economic structuring providing economic growth), transition to financial liberalisation can do more harm than good. It is necessary to have a stable growth rate if the economy desires to benefit from long term capital movements. Since grounds influencing capital movements are limited in an economy with structural and institutional weaknesses, short term capital flows enter only in high interest rates and this in return increases the risk for crisis. Short term capital flows enter for high rate of real interest to profit from interest rate arbitrage, and it leads to overvaluation of national currency while profiting excessively in the short run. Such an environment disturbs the balance between the FX rate and real interest rate and it creates an externally dependent artificial growth environment, which may lead to crisis. When crisis circumstances occur, the functions of monetary authority in central banks are gradually restricted and thus national currency is out of control (Eren and Suslu, 2001).

From the perspective of financial crisis, it is defined in the studies on the causes and indicators of crises that there are different types of indicators with respect to the type of crisis (Yay, 2001). The models used in studies are grouped under four categories (Cinko, 2008, Yay, 2001, Eren and Suslu, 2001): According to the first generation models, crises arise from incompatibility between applied macro-economic policies and a fixed exchange rate regime. These models are used in explaining the crises that occurred particularly in the 1980s in Latin American countries. In these models, overvaluation of the currency in real terms and an increase in the current account deficit are identified as the leading indicators of crisis, while failure of domestic monetary and financial policies and a serious decrease in foreign currency reserves are identified as reasons for crisis. In the second generation models, which emerged because the first generation models could not provide explanations for the crises experienced in the European monetary system in the 1990s, the domestic interest rate and amount of production are indicators of crisis, as well.

The first two models, which became inadequate in explaining the Asian crisis experienced in 1997, have been substituted by models claiming that sources of monetary and banking crises are the banking and finance sectors (Yay, 2001). In these types of models, micro-economic indicators can reflect the probability of crisis better than macro-economic indicators. Spill over effect models however, are the models which explain that, due to the integrating of world today's economies, a crisis emerging in one country can trigger crises in other places and it cannot be explained by macro-economic reasons. The interdependence of financial markets is the most important factor facilitating the spill over effect. Besides, the fact that creditors are the same, and in the case of a negative circumstance in one country, required by the rules, these institutions recall the loans given to other countries or do not revolve these loans when the loan term is reached, thereby speeding up the spread of crises (Yay, 2001).

Comprehensive research is conducted on the causes of the 1994 and 2001 crises experienced by Turkey recently. The general view on the 1994 crisis is that budget deficit is one of the most important reasons for the crisis. Due the inadequacy of domestic savings, the budget deficits were met by capital movements within the capacity provided by financial liberalisation, the low FX rate increased the trade and current account deficits, and resulted in balance of payments and budget deficit, called twin deficits. Excessive liquidity in the market and the effort to keep the domestic interest rate down to lower the borrowing cost, and the twin deficits' increase to unsustainably high levels, resulted in a loss of confidence on the ability to pay back debts and also led to crisis (Isik et al., 2001). In the studies conducted on the 2001 crisis, the causes of the crisis are listed as the fragile structure in the banking sector due to high public sector borrowing requirement and wrong policies in financing that. Besides, it is stated that as a result of the overvaluation of TL, resulting from fixed FX rate policy, consumption increased, imports increased and the increasing current account deficit was a significant reason in the formation of the crisis (Yay, 2001). In a more comprehensive study on the period 1929-2001, the causes of crises are identified as including both external and internal factors (Kazgan, 2009):

External Factors

Characteristics of External Factors: It is the characteristic of international incident and financial liberty and the hot money movements after 1990 that they had more impact on developing countries like Turkey with an outward-oriented policy.

How External Factors Influence: As the dependency on overseas countries increases, the rate of effectiveness for external factors increases and no room remains for a country to intervene in the domestic market. The influences of external factors are listed below:

a) Large reversals in foreign trade rate,
b) Devaluation of export markets or competitive currencies,
c) Stagnation in export markets or in big countries,
d) Rapid increase in global or regional interest rates,
e) Outflow of hot money: Expectation of devaluation due to current account deficit and increase in debt or the possibility of higher returns in another market outside the country lead capital outflow. Capital outflows cause a devaluation of TL, a decrease in reserves, a narrowing of the money supply, an increase in interest rates, the shifting of financial placements to foreign currency and interest, and following that, the collapse of the stock exchange. With the further increase in the interest rates by the state in order to stop demand for foreign currency, the real manufacturing sector are influenced due to shrinking demand and companies are influenced by such developments proportionate to their debt burden and the shrink in the markets. Such developments result in a decrease in production and employment. Increasing indebtedness prevents Turkey from coming up with solutions to the crisis through expansionist policies (with Keynesian spending increasing measures) and it was the restriction of public spending (due to the IMF program) and the Central Bank that caused the collapse of the domestic demand and deepened the crisis by not printing money in the 2000-2001 crisis.

Internal Factors

Role of Economic Policies: It is stated that a planned mixed economy is the most effective economic policy both in preventing and overcoming crises more easily. Turkey had tightly applied planned economic policies in the 1930s and 1961-74. For Turkey, macro-economic stability was protected, the economy grew and industrialisation materialised in these periods. The crisis in the period 1969-70 however was overcome through a mild devaluation. Further negative effects that could come from the world economy were avoided without much damage. The 1950s are an example of the transition to a free market economy by an unprepared economy, and economic liberties Turkey planned to implement collapsed after 1954, and loosing functionality, the free market economy faced crisis. The Turkish economy grew after liberalised goods and services markets with post-1950 capital movements, but in return, domestic and foreign debts, current account deficit and financial vulnerability increased.

Current Account Deficit: Liberalisation of the capital movements is the main cause in the overvaluation of TL through capital inflows and increasing current account deficits. Current account deficits were generally met through short term foreign debt. In the period when capital movements were controlled, due to a draw back in foreign debt and increase in import restrictions as preventive measures (as in 1954-58 or 1978-79), current account deficit decreased, and there was a fall in price increases and the import of raw material or intermediate product due to decrease in supply resulted reductions in production. Inability to practice this after the liberalisation of the capital movements, and a change in the direction of the hot money or activity in foreign exchange became the main reasons triggering the crisis.

Domestic and External Public Debt: Borrowing for public deficits met by foreign debt with high interest rate from the banks creates public debts through borrowing with high interest, and it makes the commercial banking system fragile. A rise in the interest of the credit or inability to renew foreign debt during growth in foreign debt, or such an expectation is another crucial factor triggering the crisis. Crisis also leads an increase in the public debt. In the 1990s and during the bank collapses in 2000-2002, obligations of the banks overtaken by the state led to an increase in public debts. Besides, while foreign exchange that increases during crisis led an increase in the TL provisions of foreign debts and interest rates, they also led an increase in the interest expense of domestic debts. In order to stop the increase in foreign exchange, the remaining instruments in financial liberalisation are interest rates and state borrowing at extremely high interest rates and efforts to stop such increases.

External Debts of the Banks and Companies: Parallel to the increases in current account deficit, rapid increases in external debt have been observed. The majority of them are private debts. External debts have been growing with renewals and they can turn into a structure where lenders' risks increase. Inability to pay back the interest of borrowed loans causes crisis. Decline in the economy and increasing unemployment shrink domestic demand, and increasing interest and foreign currency prices lead to a decrease in the imports, creating an incentive for exports and leading to current account surplus. This results in the decrease in debt stocks. Inability to pay back the loans (as in 1958 and before the agreement with the IMF in 1978) can lead to the point of declaring moratorium. After liberalisation of the capital movements, mismanagement of public and private institutions can become a main factor disrupting the financial balances of the country.

Macro-economic Instability: All crisis models consist of various crisis indicators. Leading indicators of financial crisis are stated as overvaluation of the real foreign exchange rate, increase in the M2 money supply to foreign currency reserves ratio, increasing current deficit/GDP ratio (rising above 4%), extreme expansion of loan volume, fluctuations in foreign exchange rates, extreme rises in overnight interest rates, and excessive decreases in foreign currency reserves (Cinko, 2008, Eren and Suslu, 2001). Regarding crisis indicators, there are many studies in the literature. Some of them are listed below for reference:

Macro-Economic Indicators (Cinko, 2008):

1. Real Interest Rate
2. Real FX Rate
3. Consolidated Budget
4. Current Account Deficit
5. Foreign Currency Reserves
6. Trade Deficit
7. Export/Import Ratio
8. Growth Rate
9. Inflation
10. Capacity Utilisation Rate
11. Unemployment Rate

Financial Indicators (Cinko, 2008):

1. Private Sector Loans/GDP
2. Loan Expansion Rate
3. Short Term Capital Movement/GDP
4. M2/Foreign Currency Reserves
5. Total Domestic Debt/M2Y
6. Commercial Bank Reserves/Total Reserves
7. Total Deposits
8. Total Foreign Currency Deposits
9. Foreign Currency Liabilities of Commercial Banks/GDP
10. Banking Sector Open Position

Variables used in another study to determine leading indicators of crisis in the Turkish economy are given below (Isik et al., 2004):

1. Budget Deficit/GNP
2. Public Sector Borrowing Requirement/GNP
3. Current Account Deficit/GNP
4. Current Account Deficit/Central Bank Foreign Currency Reserves
5. Current Account Deficit/International Foreign Currency Reserves
6. M2YR/Central Bank Foreign Currency Reserves (M2YR=M2+Foreign Currency Accounts+Repo)
7. M2YR/International Foreign Currency Reserves
8. M1YRS/Central Bank Foreign Currency Reserves (M1YRS: M1+Demand Deposit Accounts (FX)+Repo+Foreign or Domestic Foreign Currency Savings Accounts with A Term of One Month or Shorter)
9. M1YRS/International Foreign Currency Reserves
10. FX Demand Deposit Accounts of Banking System/Total Deposits
11. Total Loans of Banking System/International Foreign Currency Reserves
12. Foreign Assets of Banking System/Foreign Liabilities
13. Real Loan Increase Rate of Banking System
14. M2/International Foreign Currency Reserves
15. Total Loans of Banking System/GNP
16. Real Interbank Overnight Interest Rates
17. T-Bills Real Average Compound Interest Rate
18. Short Term Capital Movements
19. Portfolio Investments
20. Real Growth Rate of Economy
21. Unemployment Rate

22. ISE 100 Index
23. Real FX Rate Index

Leading macro-economic indicators in another study to forecast leading indicators of the crisis in Turkey in November 2000 and February 2001 are listed below (Karacor and Alptekin, 2006):

1. International Reserves
2. Exports
3. Foreign Trade Rate
4. Real FX Rate
5. M1 Level
6. M2/Reserve Currency multiplier
7. Domestic Loans/GDP
8. Real Deposit Interest Rate Progress
9. M2/Gross International Reserves
10. Manufacturing Index

Indicators giving consistent results and used extensively in forecasting monetary and banking crises are defined as real foreign exchange rate, domestic loan expansion, and M2/International Reserve rate. However, 23 variables have been determined in a study conducted on Turkey and they are listed below (Ural, 2003):

1. Imports Growth Rate
2. Change in Real FX Rate
3. Trade Deficit/GDP
4. Foreign Assets/Foreign Liabilities
5. M2/Reserves
6. Total Deposits/GDP
7. M2/GDP
8. Deposits Real Interest Rate
9. Domestic Loans/GDP
10. Real GDP Growth Rate
11. Industry Manufacturing Index
12. Inflation Rate
13. International Reserves/GDP
14. Reserves/Imports
15. Short Term Capital Movements
16. Foreign Currency Interest Rate
17. Oil Prices Increase Rate

18. Budget Deficit/GDP
19. Total Debt/GDP
20. Political Risk
21. Financial Risk
22. Corruption
23. Law and Order

The crisis indicators obtained in various categories in another study on crisis models in the world are given below (Yay, 2001):

Macro-economic Indicators:
1. Inflation
2. Public Deficits/GNP
3. Investment/GNP
4. Investment Increase Rate/GNP
5. Real GNP Increase Rate
6. Difference with respect to US Interest Rates
7. Capital Controls
8. Regional Spill Over Indicators

Financial Indicators:
1. Rate of Increase in Domestic Loans
2. Increase in Loans to Private Sector/GNP Increase
3. CB Loans to Banks/GNP
4. Changes in Money Multiplier
5. M2/International Reserves
6. M2/GNP
7. International Reserves/Imports
8. Changes in Interest Rates
9. Increase of Private Sector Liabilities

Indicators for Current Accounts and Debts:
1. Balance of Trade
2. Foreign Trade Rates
3. Current Account Deficit/GNP
4. Export Increase Rate
5. Exports/GNP
6. Imports/GNP
7. Exports+Imports/GNP
8. Rate of Real FX Rate Revaluation
9. Total Debt/GNP

10. Debt Service/GNP
11. Short Term Debt/Total Debt
12. Short Term External Debt/International Reserve
13. Total Debt/International Reserve
14. Total Debt/Exports
15. Debts Service/Exports
16. Interest Payments/Exports
17. Public Debt/Total Debt
18. Foreign Direct Investments/Total Debt

Micro-economic Indicators (Related to the Banking Sector):

1. Uncollectable Debts/Total Debt
2. Total Debt/Assets
3. Capital/Assets
4. Interest Income/Assets
5. Operational Expenses/Assets
6. Profits/Assets

All the indicators mentioned above are the indicators used in studies forecasting the causes of crises in Turkey and the world, and studies are conducted to forecast the financial crises regarding the status of the indicators determined with respect to certain behaviours or threshold values. Due to the fact that, in times of crisis the values of such indicators differ from their normal progress, they are significant values in determining the measures to avoid crisis. In the book, the values of macro-economic variables in periods of crisis in Turkey have been assessed from a dependency perspective.

CHAPTER FIVE

ASSESSING THE ECONOMY OF THE TURKISH REPUBLIC IN 1923-1980 PERIOD

Turkey has implemented various economic models showing differences in each period. These differences have been shaped by political developments in the world and Turkey's desires and needs, and they are defined as five main periods in general (Ertuna, 2007, p. 47):

a. Liberal National Economy Period (1923–1929)
b. Development Period Under State Leadership (1929-1950)
   - Ataturk Era (1929-1938)
   - Inonu Era (1938-1950)
c. Liberal Economy Trial Period (1950-1960)
d. Planned Economy Period (1960-1980)
e. Period of Integration with Global Economy (Post-1980: Since economic model and developments after 1980 are mentioned in detail in Chapter Three, they will not be elaborated again in this chapter).

Before making a comparison of the aforementioned periods in terms of economic data, structure of the economic thinking particularly in the first years of the Republic's establishment, meaning economic policy of Ataturk, and clarifying the fundamentals is crucial in analysing the data in order to define the bases on which consequences of the economic policies relied.

Economic Policy of Ataturk

The political thought which was dominant in the first years of the establishment of the Republic came into prominence in the field of economics, and financial independence principle was primary in economic policies until the 1950s. In these policies formed by Ataturk, the bad heritage from the Ottoman Empire had a significant share. The Ottoman Empire turning into a colony, economically speaking, its inability to develop industry and make politically independent decisions due to external debts, led the founding cadre of Republic to draw important lessons, and with a rational structure, they based all their policies on such lessons drawn from the failures of the past. Two main reasons why industry did not develop in the Ottoman Empire are as follows:

Capitulations/Free Trade Agreements: Capitulations, which are defined as implementing low or zero customs reciprocally between two states or in other words free trade agreements, became an important problem in the declining period of the Empire due to industrial revolution in Europe (Tunc, 2009). Except for the United Kingdom, which realised the Industrial Revolution first, all other developed countries became industrialised behind the walls of protection and began to defend the idea of free trade. Because they were at the bottom of the ladder in terms of Industrial Revolution, France, Germany, Austria and the USA prevented British goods from entering their countries through high customs taxes in order to protect their national markets (Sabir, 2006). The Ottoman Empire started free trade with United Kingdom with the signing of the Baltalimani Trade Agreement on 18th August 1838 and with this agreement the Ottoman State based its economic policy on completely free trade (Sabir, 2006). The result of free trade policy was that mass produced cheap goods resulting from the Industrial Revolution entered the Empire through low taxes and trade centres in the coastal cities, and this led to further decrease in local production and Ottoman industry, comprised of hand looms and mid-sized enterprises, which collapsed at the very beginning due to encountering the competition of Western product.

Barriers for capital accumulation: Capital accumulation, a precondition of industrialisation, could not be ensured in the Ottoman Empire. The reason was the mentality of the state opposing capital accumulation or enrichment of the citizens. According to that, in the name of the Sultan, the state has the right to confiscate the belongings of anybody living in the borders of the Empire (except Sheikh al-Islam). By using this right, the state confiscated the belongings of institutions and enriched people (Tunc, 2009). Most of the time, the assets obtained by a landed proprietor–notable class enriched by land purchases were confiscated, but with the Imperial Edict of Reorganisation *(Tanzimat Fermani)* declared in 1839, the property right was guaranteed. This method, which can be called capital distribution rather than capital accumulation, also hindered the emergence of a strong candidate for dynasty. However, due to this approach, the Ottoman bourgeoisie could not emerge. Furthermore, since the state was not active and industrial bourgeoisie was not available, it was only the other states who invested in Ottoman industry. Instead of making investments in other countries, they aimed to sell the industrial goods through intermediaries with low taxes via capitulations, particularly in the coastal harbour cities, and instead of a national bourgeoisie, it led to bourgeoisie mainly formed by minorities, namely comprador bourgeoisie.

One of the biggest problems in the last period of the Ottoman Empire was the budget deficit and related to that, external debt. Products of the machinery industry entering the Empire without custom tax resulted in the wiping out of the Ottoman Empire's industry in its infancy within a very short period of time, and led to much more import than export; when it was combined with wars, it created large financing deficits and a borrowing dependant country (Celebi, 2002). In the Empire on the edge of bankruptcy after the end of 18th Century, the first foreign debt occurred during the Crimean War in 1854. In the Empire, declared moratorium in 1875 and became unable to pay back its debts, an institution called the Ottoman Public Debt Administration *(Duyun-u Umumiye)* was established for the collection of the receivables by lenders. In order to pay back the debts, this institution had authority to collect the state taxes on salt and tobacco monopolies, stamp duty, taxes received from fishery and alcoholic beverages, the tithe *(osur)* on raw silk and the annual tax paid by the State of Eastern Rumelia. In this way, tax collection, which is one of the most important provisions of state formation, was transferred to an institution in favour of other countries (Pamuk, 2008, p. 121).

In its simplest terms, these developments are stated by Parvus Effendi in the journal of Turk Yurdu (Turkish Homeland) on 18 October 1912 (Celebi, 2002) as follows:

> Thanks to its nationalistic finance, Europe has been forcing the Ottoman State into huge debts and it has been putting the State under its enslavement from economics and politics perspective. With the big blows, it strikes from outside, Europe has been devastating the Independence of the Ottoman State and also through the commercial and financial activities carried inside, it has been turning the Empire into a colony of capital owners.

The heritage passed from the Ottoman Empire to the Turkish Republic was poverty, external dependency due to the lack of local industry, external debt, and an economy with no production (Sabir, 2006). As mentioned in the previous chapter, capital accumulation in the country, in other words having a Turkish bourgeoisie to invest, could not be formed. In the Ottoman era, trade was largely under the monopoly of Greek, Armenian and Jewish minorities (Sabir, 2006).

In light of all of this, the belief that independence gained after national struggle should be supported by financial independence was promoted. During Lausanne negotiations, the words of Lord Curzon to Ismet Inonu which were *"Whatever we want, you reject. Now we are putting them into our pockets but you are a poor country that just came out of war. You will need money for development. When you come to us for this in the future we will bring them in front of you and we will get them"*, are notable since they reflect the underlying reason on why the economic policy of the first years of the Republic targeted a fully independent economic structure (Ertuna, 2007, p. 48).

In the opening speech of the Izmir Economics Congress on the 22th of February 1923, Ataturk clearly voiced sovereignty in financial terms as well (Sabir, 2006, Aysan, 1980, p. 21, Celebi, 2002):

> There is one reality left over from the filter of history and experience. If Turkish history is analysed it will be observed that the reasons for decline and collapse are linked to economic problems. All the victories and failures are related to economic conditions. Our nation has devastated enemy armies. For full independence, there exists the following rule: National sovereignty should be supported by financial sovereignty. The force that will take us to this target is the economy. No matter how great the political and military victories are, without crowned with economic victory, they cannot be long-lasting.
>
> There is no civilised state which does not consider its economy before its army and navy. Full independence surely means independence in all areas like politics, finance, economics, justice, military and culture and full freedom. Lack of independence in any of the ones I cited means that nation and state is lack of full independence. The objective of our wars at present is full independence. And full independence is only possible with financial independence.
>
> For full independence there exists this principle: National sovereignty should be strengthened with economic sovereignty.

The dominant economic thought in the first years of the Republic was that of predicating the market mechanism on capital accumulation, which materialised through the private sector, and the basic meaning of the national economy was interpreted as the transfer of economic powers from the hands of foreigners and minorities before the national independence war to local tradesmen, meaning building a local bourgeoisie (Sabir, 2006,

Ozcelik and Tuncer, 2007). As a result of this, in Izmir Economics Congress, an agreement was concluded on an economic model which was predominantly private sector and market economy oriented, and an "Economic Pact" was defined (Sabir, 20006, Ozcelik and Tuncer, 2007). In the decisions of Izmir Economics Congress, the main duty of the state was defined as largely infrastructure related, and the establishment of railway and road networks, building of harbours, the establishment of telecommunications infrastructure and assuming educational affairs were planned. It was decided to found commercial and industrial banks and to lead joint ventures, then to transfer them to the private sector. It was planned that the state should not follow *"laissez faire, laissez passer" (let them do, let them go)* and should not be an important player in the economic domain, either (Sabir, 2006, Celebi, 2002).

One of the determinant factors of this period was also the financial provisions of the Lausanne Agreement. Capitulations were lifted in the Lausanne Agreement. Although it was a great achievement to lift the capitulations, a large portion of Ottoman debts were left to Turkey. In the agreement signed between Turkey and lender countries on the 13th of June 1928, Turkey pledged to pay 107 million gold lira of 161 million gold lira debts. Another important article was about customs tax and independent foreign trade was restricted in the article. In the Trade Agreement signed as an annex to the Lausanne Agreement, it was mentioned that for a five year period and with some exceptions, import and export restrictions should be lifted, they should not be replaced by new ones, and custom tax rates should stay the same for five years (Boratav, 2009, p. 44, Ugur, 2007). According to the Agreement, Turkey pledged to keep the customs tax rates for the goods imported from England, France, Italy, Japan, Greece, Yugoslavia and Romania at the 1916 Ottoman rate (Ozcelik and Tuncer, 2007). Considering all of these factors, it is a matter for discussion whether the transition to a planned economy policy and statism after 1929 was an obligation or whether there was a need to implement a new program (Sabir, 2006). With the planned economy in use, Turkey was the first country among the democratic countries experiencing a planned economy in the world. The opportunities generated by the 1929 financial crisis (a suitable economic environment to nationalise the foreign companies and monopolies) and implementing the termination of financial provisions of the Lausanne Agreement (especially articles putting restrictions on customs) created an impression that an infrastructure was already present.

The main objective of Ataturk was to realise economic development as soon as possible and it is noted that economic policy is based on three fundamental balances (Sabir, 2006, Aysan, 1980, p. 49, 89):

1. A financial policy with equal income and expenses for domestically strong state treasury (Balanced Budget),
2. Balanced TL preventing inflation; a well-functioning banking system, a monetary policy with equal resources and expenses,
3. A Foreign Economic Relations Policy protecting the strength of the State Treasury in foreign economic relations, protecting TL's value against foreign currencies and aimed at increasing this value, with equal revenue and expense of the foreign currency (Balance of Trade or Foreign Trade Surplus).

In terms of finance i.e., budget, due to the common belief that foreign borrowing and depreciation in the value of money are the consequences of budget deficits; budget balance or surplus was promoted as a principle to protect relentlessly in the economic policy of Ataturk (Aysan, 1980, p. 31). In the opening speech of Ataturk on the 1st of November 1933, the emphasis on this matter is reflected as follows (THS, 1961, p. 374):

> ... I am sure that in order to reach and maintain budget balance in all circumstances, your high committee will pay special attention on taking all necessary precautions. The Great National Assembly, aware of the uncalculated drawbacks of a budget with deficit, dedicated to balanced budget is great collateral for the financial and yet general policy of the state.

It was targeted to improve state revenues through an increase in public income, and a financial system based on lifting the taxes negatively influencing production and economic life. The best example illustrating this is the lifting of the tithe *(osur in Turkish)* tax extensively influencing the agricultural sector in 1925.

Ataturk, emphasising reliable monetary policy as one of the substantial factors of the strong economy, had always been opposed to printing money with no backing i.e., deficit financing, and he refused deficit financing and inflationist policies including the time period of the Independence War (Sabir, 2006, Celebi, 2002, Aysan, 1980, p. 32). No commodity backing of printed money i.e., monetary volume expansion more than growth, leads to an increase in demand disrupting the supply-demand equilibrium and hinders investments due to inflation. Besides, high increase in demand leads to disequilibrium in trade balance due to an increase in imports, and inflation disrupts disequilibrium in income distribution (Sabir, 2006).

The aim was for state expenditures met by tax revenues instead of printing money in order not to cause inflation and for a reliable and strong currency. Mentioned in the previous chapter, this means a balanced budget. Since there is no capacity to keep the value of TL constant against foreign currencies without balanced state budget and a monetary policy without inflation, Ataturk continuously emphasised the balanced budget and strong currency (Aysan, 1980, p. 55). In the opening speech on the 1st of November 1936 (THS, 1961, p. 390) his statement that; *"...Keeping our treasury strong in the years ahead will be your most important job. Current stability of our national currency will be protected"* and his speech at the opening on the 1st November 1938 that *"Our Finance Ministry has been following the principles of balanced budget, strong payment, improvement of the tax system and lightening the burden on tax payers and protecting the stability of national currency with extensive loyalty and success"* clearly shows the emphasis on balanced budget and stable monetary policy (anti-inflationist) by Ataturk (the 1st of November 1938 speech was read by Celal Bayar at the Grand National Assembly of Turkey due to Ataturk's illness).

After the bad experiences concerning foreign borrowing in the years of Ottoman Empire, Ataturk was opposed to spending the money received through foreign borrowing on public or private consumption. Moreover, the most important target in foreign trade was equal exports and imports, or exports being higher than imports and creating reserves. In his statements in the opening speech on 1st of November 1937 (THS, 1961, p. 395-396) that; *"The main principle we follow in foreign trade is to maintain the active character of our trade balance. Because, it constitutes the most important base in Turkish balance of payment"* he referred to the emphasis of a trade balance or even surplus, and mentioned it as a condition for full independence. Savings through lowering consumption of domestic goods was perceived as an important pillar and instrument. Thereby, an aim is to support local production and generate a trade surplus through savings, enabling necessary reserves for investments requiring high capital expenditure (Celebi, 2002, Aysan, 1980, p. 64).

One of the most important economic policies of Ataturk is industrialisation and statist policies. In the Ataturk period, state resources were allocated for domestic affairs, justice, national defence, foreign relations and national education, called primary duties of the state. In relation to this, general and supplementary budget revenues were allocated for the basic functions and the remaining amounts and borrowings were used for large investments. Priority investment fields were agricultural and infrastructural investments. Ataturk objected to foreign capital ownership particularly in infrastructure, mining and primary areas of the public works (Aysan, 1980, p. 68).

As mentioned in previous chapters, while the free market economic model was used for development and industrialisation until 1929, statist policies were promoted. In transition to statist policies, while the crisis experienced in the world had some influence, unrealised industrial investments by liberal policies between 1923 and 1929 also had a crucial impact (Rozaliyev, 1978, p. 77). Ataturk, in a note he passed to Celal Bayar at the opening ceremony of the Izmir International Fair in 1935, clearly stated what he meant by statist policy (Aysan, 1980, p. 6):

> Statist system Turkey has been applying is not a system which was taken and translated from thoughts that socialist theoreticians have claimed since the 19th century. This is a system that emerged from Turkey's needs and is specific to Turkey. For us, the meaning of statism is the following: Prioritising activities of the individuals, but taking the economy of the country in the hands of the state considering the necessities of the country and the fact that several things have not been achieved yet.

Regarding this model, called mild statism by Ataturk and Inonu, grounds for such a principle are clearly stated by Inonu at a ceremony dated 30th of August 1930 to celebrate the railway reaching Sivas (Aysan, 1980, s. 47):

> A theory of liberalism is something that this country can hardly understand. We are really mild statist in economics. What directed us to this direction is the necessity in the country and national tendency. For the needs of the country, everybody and every place ask for help from the Treasury. A city without electricity, the place with a bad harbour, a man who cannot find a job comes to the government. Being mild statist, we have misconduct because we cannot catch up with development inclinations and thoughts. Giving up statism and expecting every blessing from the activities of the capital owner, is this something this country can understand?

Statism was included in the constitution with law no 3115 on the 5th of February 1937. Objectives of the policy are listed as economic independence and fast development in general (Sabir, 2006). Factors forming statist policy are grouped under four categories (Ozcelik and Tuncer, 2007):

- The fact that liberal economy policies in 1923-1929 did not generate desired results,
- Negative effects of the 1929 Great Depression,
- Successful results of planned economic policies in the USSR,
- Liberal economic policies' inability to come up with a solution for the 1929 depression.

Although the world economic crisis in 1929 had a negative effect on Turkey, it was limited, compared to other countries. The most important reason is the low level of integration with the world and economic policies based on three balances (Celebi, 2002). Generally speaking, in the economic policies that were restrictive in nature, implementations to expand the economy were realised by statist policies. The actual implementation started with the first Five Year Development Plan (FYDP). The main objectives of the first FYDP are as follows (Inan, 1972, p. 16):

1. The branches of the industry with main raw materials provided domestically or easily will be focused.
2. Because the factories planned are the factories requiring large capital or technical power, their establishment will be left to the state institutions.
3. Production capacities of factories planned will be parallel to necessity and consumption.

Within the framework of the plan and statist policy, it was planned to move under the guidance and protection of the state in order to make huge investments for the public by the state and with a plan, to keep the private sector from misspending and to work in parallel with the national interests (Inan, 1972, p. 17). The most significant element of statist policy and industrialisation is defined as State Economic Enterprises (SEE) which would conduct investments. Basic principles to achieve the goals in the plan are defined in parallel to the objectives set during the establishment of the SEEs (Aysan, 1980, p. 81-82):

1. SEEs are investment and financing institutions, and they are defined as institutions making investments and providing financing.
2. SEEs will work just like a company with market economy rules.
3. SEEs will invest in areas where private sector is not willing due to lack of capital, lack of technical or managerial intelligence.

4. As private sector improves, SEEs, with temporary economic stance, will withdraw from these areas and invest in other areas.

The first SEE established within such a development model as an example was Sumerbank (Aysan, 1980, p. 77). In the first FYDP, investments in five sectors, namely weaving, paper, mining, ceramics and chemistry, were targeted and the total value of the investments was 44 million TL. 41.6 million would be met by Sumerbank and 2.4 million would be met by Is Bank (Tunc, 2009). Through investments, it aimed to decrease import and complete halt some branches of imports and export (Tunc, 2009). Within the framework of the first FYDP in 1933, elements of the statist policy were reflected in the establishment of the objectives of Sumerbank assigned to the establishment of Turkish industry (Ertuna, 2007, p. 49-50):

1. To eliminate the factors with negative effects on manufacturing activities,
2. To make the private sector companies work in a commercial liberty environment with rational working methods,
3. To give endurance to the industrialisation ,
4. To raise educated human resources necessary for industrialisation.

Although rational working methods and the investment in educated human resources are crucial in the economic success of the Republican period, the spirit of the Turkish Revolutionaries the statist model emphasised was a much more important driving force with generated desire for development self-confidence. Development thrust was not only economic but also a thrust with cultural and social aspects. Factories built all around Turkey with social, sporting, cultural and healthcare facilities, were formed as pioneering institutions in the development of their regions (Ertuna, 2007, p. 50).

Liberal National Economy Period (1923–1929)

As explained in detail in the previous section, Turkey adopted a liberal economic system in this period as well. Despite this, because of what was experienced before and during the establishment of the Republic as well as political concerns, foreign borrowing was avoided, foreign capital investments were considered positively with the condition of their compliance with the sovereignty rights of the country, and all the concessions to foreign capital were rejected (Cosar, 1996a).

A determinant factor in the economic policies of the period was that the customs tariffs applied by Turkey to other countries would be the tariffs of 1916 for the next five years, starting from the signature date, according to the trade agreement signed as an annex to the Lausanne Agreement in 1923. Turkey could not use its sovereignty rights until 1929 in terms of customs tariffs (Ugur, 2007). Except 1927, growth was ensured in the period. The 15 million TL Gross National Product (GNP) with respect to 1990 fixed prices, reached 26.9 Million TL in 1929. It corresponds to an increase in the annual compound rate of 10.3% (Table 5-1). It is noted that there was a 4.3% annual average increase in inflation.

In this period, balanced budget was always stated as the most important target. Although the total budget gave a surplus, periodic budget deficit was only present in 1925 and the reason was the lifting of the tithe *(osur)* tax which comprised 25% of tax revenues. Although the tithe tax was substituted with various taxes, the results of the measures could only be observed in the following year; tax revenues decreased and a budget deficit occurred in 1925 (Table 5-2). The budget gave an average annual surplus of 1.4 million USD in the period. In terms of debts, balanced budget and strong currency principles in Turkey were considered as the most important principles with regards to economic and financial policy (Cosar, 1996a). For this reason, no domestic or external borrowing was made in period 1923-1929.

Table 5-1 Main Macro Economic Figures in Period 1923-1929 (SSI, 2001, Pakdemirli, 2003)

Years	GNP (Million TL-1990 Constant)	GNP (Million USD)	GNP Increase (%-1990 Constant)	USD FX Increase (% Real)	Inflation (CPI %-December)
1923	14.94	826.11	0.0	0.0	9.0
1924	17.16	932.89	14.9	1.7	10.0
1925	19.29	1,214.57	12.4	-13.6	12.7
1926	22.90	1,258.97	18.7	14.5	-8.9
1927	19.89	1,104.85	-13.2	-1.1	2.7
1928	22.26	1,219.70	11.9	1.4	-0.9
1929	26.87	1,459.10	20.7	0.9	5.2

Table 5-2 Macro Economic Figures Related to Budget in Period 1923-1929 (SSI, 2001, Pakdemirli, 2003)

Years	Budget Deficit (Million USD)	Budget Deficit / Total Budget Revenue	Total Budget Revenue (Million USD)	Total Budget Expenses (Million USD)
1923	3.18	4.80	66.23	63.05
1924	3.61	4.90	73.63	70.01
1925	-16.97	-18.23	93.11	110.08
1926	4.28	4.53	94.43	90.15
1927	1.69	1.63	104.25	102.55
1928	10.72	9.41	113.86	103.15
1929	5.21	4.81	108.28	103.08

Table 5-3 Macro Economic Figures Related to Foreign Trade in Period 1923-1929 (SSI, 2001, Pakdemirli, 2003)

Years	Foreign Trade Deficit / GNP	Foreign Trade Deficit (Million USD)	Import (Million USD)	Export (Million USD)
1923	-4.4	-36.08	86.87	50.79
1924	-1.9	-18.03	100.46	82.44
1925	-2.2	-26.25	128.95	102.70
1926	-2.0	-24.97	121.41	96.44
1927	-2.4	-27.00	107.75	80.75
1928	-2.1	-25.43	113.71	88.28
1929	-3.3	-48.73	123.56	74.83

Regarding foreign trade, Turkey, not having any authority to change the customs tariffs between 1923 and 1929, continuously had trade deficits, and particularly because of the speculative imports made with the expectations on custom tariff change in 1929, the trade deficit reached its peak (Table 5-3). In the period, the average trade deficit was 29.5 Million USD, and the export/import ratio was 73.6%.

Period of Development under State Leadership (1929-1950)

Ataturk Era (1929-1938)

Due to the 1929 world economic crisis and the inability of pre-1929 liberal economic policies to meet expectations, Turkey started implementing statist policies, changed the customs tariffs, and it nationalised the enterprises owned by foreign investors. Within the framework of the statist policies, Turkey began to invest in local industries that the private entrepreneurs were not able to enter in the period 1923-1929; within this scope, Sumerbank and Etibank were established and these institutions became the pioneers of industrialism in Turkey and encouraged production and use of domestic production. Because of the policy changes in 1929, 1929 is the year that calculations in this chapter were made.

Except for 1932 and 1935, the economy grew throughout the period. With respect to 1990 fixed prices, GNP which was approximately 22.3 Million TL at the beginning of 1929 reached 43.7 Million TL in 1938. This corresponds to an increase in the annual compound average of 7.0% (Table 5-4). However, regarding inflation, an annual average decrease of 4.4% is observed.

Table 5-4 Main Macro Economic Figures in Period 1930-1938 (SSI, 2001, Pakdemirli, 2003)

Years	GNP (Million TL-1990 Constant)	GNP (Million USD)	GNP Increase (%-1990 Constant)	USD FX Increase (% Real)	Inflation (CPI %-December)
1929	26.87	1,459.10	20.7	0.9	5.2
1930	27.54	1,061.13	2.50	40.94	-25.62
1931	29.89	960.87	8.55	19.88	-18.89
1932	26.62	808.69	10.96	5.80	-5.48
1933	30.86	1,001.76	15.94	-6.41	-15.94
1934	32.88	1,406.15	6.54	-24.10	0.00
1935	32.10	1,514.73	-2.38	-9.38	10.34
1936	39.09	1,959.90	21.78	-5.88	6.25
1937	39.90	2,088.82	2.07	-4.23	4.41
1938	43.71	2,157.71	9.57	6.07	-4.23

Table 5-5 Macro Economic Figures Related to Budget in Period 1930-1938 (SSI, 2001, Pakdemirli, 2003)

Years	Budget Deficit (Million USD)	Budget Deficit / Total Budget Revenue	Total Budget Revenue (Million USD)	Total Budget Expenses (Million USD)
1929	5.21	4.81	108.28	103.08
1930	3.37	3.37	100.21	96.83
1931	-7.88	-10.07	78.31	86.19
1932	-11.94	-13.49	88.54	100.48
1933	0.41	0.39	105.00	104.58
1934	-17.13	-10.41	164.51	181.63
1935	-22.38	-12.19	183.64	206.02
1936	14.82	6.89	215.14	200.32
1937	21.42	8.59	249.34	227.92
1938	14.88	5.90	252.29	237.41

In the budget structure, although balanced budget was always stated as the most important target, the years after 1931 were the years in which budget deficits appeared due to nationalisation and recently established SOEs. Despite investments, average budget deficit was 0.1 million USD annually (Table 5-5).

Due to nationalisation and financial requirements arising from SOEs, Turkey leaned heavily towards internal borrowing. External debt was used in correlation with investments (Table 5-6). External debts after then also included the debts which Turkey would pay as per the requirement of the agreement signed in 1933, as a result of repeated negotiations caused by the inability to pay the Ottoman debts agreement due to the economic crisis in the world and which was made after the Lausanne Agreement in 1928 (Cosar, 1996c).

After 1929, changing customs tariffs of Turkey and promoting domestic production and its use by the state instead of the goods provided from abroad within the framework of the statist policy, foreign trade began to give surplus after 1930. In the period, the annual average trade surplus was 7.5 Million USD and the export/import ratio was 112% (Table 5-7).

Table 5-6 Macro Economic Figures Related to Indebtedness in Period 1930-1938 (SSI, 2001, Pakdemirli, 2003)

	(Million USD)				
Years	Total Debt	Domestic Debt	External Debt	Debt Remaining from the Ottoman Empire	Total Debt / GNP
1929	0	0	0	-	0.00
1930	0	0	0	-	0.00
1931	0	0	0	-	0.00
1932	47	0	47	-	5.75
1933	210	120	89	48	20.94
1934	357	175	182	59	25.36
1935	379	190	189	54	25.05
1936	395	198	197	49	20.18
1937	401	238	163	45	19.20
1938	420	273	146	40	19.46

Table 5-7 Macro Economic Figures Related to Foreign Trade in Period 1930-1938 (SSI, 2001, Pakdemirli, 2003)

Years	Foreign Trade Deficit / GNP	Foreign Trade Deficit (Million USD)	Import (Million USD)	Export (Million USD)
1929	-3.3	-48.73	123.56	74.83
1930	0.2	1.84	69.54	71.38
1931	0.0	0.29	59.94	60.23
1932	0.9	7.25	40.72	47.97
1933	1.3	12.97	45.09	58.07
1934	0.3	4.25	68.76	73.01
1935	0.4	5.60	70.64	76.23
1936	1.0	20.05	73.62	93.67
1937	0.9	18.69	90.54	109.23
1938	-0.2	-3.88	118.90	115.02

Inonu Era (1938-1950)

The determinant factors of this period were World War II and political and economic developments in the post-war world. The main objectives were making all resources available for the army and ensuring the defence of the country on the eve of World War II in 1939. Thus, the state issued the National Protection Law in January 1940 in order to get economy under control through harsh security measures (Cosar, 1996b). However, these measures were not successful. A decrease in the workforce due to national mobilisation led to a decrease in production and the depletion of stocks, causing an increase in prices. In addition to this, the use of emission (printing money) for increasing expenses in war conditions was another factor that led to an increase in inflation, as well (Cosar, 1996b and 1997).

The most important change emerging in this period was that borrowing was considered as a normal income with a more positive approach by the finance administration (Cosar, 1996b and 1997). Besides, regarding budget deficits, a more flexible approach was adopted (Cosar, 1996b and 1997). This is regarded as a divergence from balanced budget, strong money and borrowing related policies which were the basic principles in the first years of the Republic.

While Turkey ranked among the Western countries in politics and economics both during the 1946-1950 post-war periods, it adopted an international free trade doctrine and by relaxing protective measures, it rearranged its foreign exchange rates. Landowners and trade bourgeoisie strengthened in the war period split from the Republican People's Party (CHP) and established the Democratic Party and after the 1947 Party Congress, the CHP abandoned statism. In this period, external debt was perceived more positively; military aid through the Truman Doctrine (1947) and economic aid through the Marshall Plan (1948) were received (Cosar, 1996b and 1997).

Table 5-8 Main Macro Economic Figures in Period 1939-1950 (SSI, 2001, Pakdemirli, 2003)

Years	GNP (Million TL-1990 Constant)	GNP (Million USD)	GNP Increase (%-1990 Constant)	USD FX Increase (% Real)	Inflation (CPI %-December)
1939	45.41	2,178.09	3.88	2.91	4.76
1940	43.11	2,537.35	-5.08	-518.52	22.73
1941	38.13	3,302.67	-11.54	-532.04	40.74
1942	41.10	6,890.76	7.79	-48.34	92.11
1943	35.20	10,267.02	-14.36	-42.52	73.97
1944	33.03	7,434.38	-6.16	29.59	-22.83
1945	28.08	6,083.23	-14.98	3.90	-3.75
1946	37.05	5,519.86	31.92	45.39	-4.96
1947	37.14	3,924.62	0.26	41.02	9.70
1948	43.48	4,939.41	17.05	-7.00	7.53
1949	38.40	4,711.25	-11.68	-7.41	8.00
1950	45.77	5,044.15	19.21	11.34	-10.19

The economic growth in this period was realised as an annual compound average of 0.4%. The economy downsized in the years during World War II grew in the post war period, however in this 11-year period, it could only rise from 43.4 million TL to 45.8 million TL with 1990 GNP fixed prices. It would be more appropriate to analyse the growth figures in terms of the war and the post-war period. When one looks at the 1939-1945 and 1946-1950 periods separately, the growth rates were realised as 2.0% and 10.3%, respectively. Starting from 1939, inflation also rapidly increased with the effects of the war and although it progressed negatively in the post war period, it was 18.1% on average for the period (Table 5-8).

When one looks at the budget figures of this period, it is observed that generally speaking balanced budget politics was kept, despite approval of deficit budgets after 1947; the budget still gave an annual average budget surplus of 17 million USD in practice (Table 5-9). This situation points to the fact that although political and economic understandings changed after the war, executive staff had not given up their habits and hesitations arising from the first years of the Republic.

It is noted that domestic debts in this period increased particularly in the war period and decreased after the war. This decrease is caused by an increase in the USD foreign exchange rate; there was no decrease in the current figures (Table 5-10).

Table 5-9 Macro Economic Figures Related to Budget in Period 1939-1950 (SSI, 2001, Pakdemirli, 2003)

Years	Budget Deficit (Million USD)	Budget Deficit / Total Budget Revenue	Total Revenue (Million USD)	Total Expenses (Million USD)
1939	1.81	0.64	282.41	280.60
1940	10.39	2.61	398.70	388.31
1941	55.70	11.34	491.00	435.30
1942	71.02	9.51	746.67	675.65
1943	9.51	1.21	787.40	777.89
1944	-46.03	-5.93	776.45	822.49
1945	44.34	8.82	502.87	458.53
1946	12.51	2.17	575.41	562.90
1947	18.14	3.14	576.79	558.66
1948	23.54	4.49	524.18	500.64
1949	20.06	3.45	581.49	561.43
1950	-17.12	-3.38	506.95	524.07

Table 5-10 Macro Economic Figures Related to Indebtedness in Period 1939-1950 (SSI, 2001, Pakdemirli, 2003)

Years	Total Debt (Million USD)	Domestic Debt (Million USD)	External Debt (Million USD)	Total Debt/ GNP
1939	451.86	289.86	162.00	20.75
1940	615.12	362.32	252.80	24.24
1941	809.65	545.45	264.20	24.52
1942	1,006.02	732.82	273.20	14.60
1943	1,063.16	786.26	276.90	10.36
1944	1,126.53	824.43	302.10	15.15
1945	1,116.69	839.69	277.00	18.36
1946	875.73	607.73	268.00	15.87
1947	614.14	357.14	257.00	15.65
1948	874.43	571.43	303.00	17.70
1949	749.00	500.00	249.00	15.90
1950	919.86	642.86	277.00	18.24

Table 5-11 Macro Economic Figures Related to Foreign Trade in Period 1939-1950 (SSI, 2001, Pakdemirli, 2003)

Years	Foreign Trade Deficit / GNP	Foreign Trade Deficit (Million USD)	Import (Million USD)	Export (Million USD)
1939	0.3	7.15	92.50	99.65
1940	1.2	30.87	50.04	80.90
1941	1.1	35.71	55.35	91.06
1942	0.2	13.24	112.88	126.12
1943	0.4	41.39	155.34	196.73
1944	0.7	51.72	126.23	177.95
1945	1.2	71.30	96.97	168.26
1946	1.7	95.69	118.89	214.58
1947	-0.5	-21.34	244.64	223.30
1948	-1.6	-78.25	275.05	196.80
1949	-0.9	-42.40	290.22	247.83
1950	-0.4	-22.24	285.66	263.42

Regarding foreign trade, when the figures of the period are observed, it is noted that there was a trade surplus with annual average of 15.2 million USD; export coverage ratio of imports (export/import ratio) was 125.6 %. However, the most important development in this period was that, when Turkey adopted international free trade doctrine after the war and relaxed protective measures, it began to give trade deficits. In the war period between 1939-1945, while the export coverage rate of imports was 136.5% and the average trade surplus was 35.9 million USD, the same figures in the post-war period of 1946-1950 were 94.4% and -13.7 Million USD, respectively (Table 5-11).

Liberal Economy Trial Period (1950–1960)

After World War II, the statist policy was discussed within the RPP, the agricultural and urban bourgeoisie classes, strengthened due to an increase in accumulation of wealth in war times, started to discuss the weight of the state in the economy. These circles, strengthened due to the increasing effect of the state by statist policy particularly after 1929, sensitivity on balanced budget and foreign borrowing, and the private sector's inability to develop sufficiently, started to voice that the weight of the state in the economy and bureaucracy should be decreased (Cosar, 2005). After the first FYDP in 1933, the second FYDP in 1938 could not be implemented due to World War II, the second FYDP projecting the establishment of basic industry was left and in order to benefit from the Marshall Plan under the leadership of the private sector, a growth policy based on the branches of light industry and agriculture was planned (Cosar, 2005).

In these periods, new economic and financial thoughts, such as the idea that no planning was necessary and borrowing was one of the revenue items in the budget, completely opposite to earlier periods, were dominant.

Although the goal of DP was restricting the weight of the state in the economy, it aimed at a development based on increase in public investments and an improvement in the private sector, and adopted a policy based on foreign aid and capital. However, because of the externally dependent industry and production becoming dependent on foreign borrowing as a result of unplanned investments, finding external debt became the most important factor of stability but in a situation when adequate sources could not be found, the economy was lured into crisis. The country became dependent on imports and external sources (Cosar, 2005). The DP expected an increase in aid for Turkey by supporting US policies unconditionally. However in 1955, the USA advised Turkey put down the development program, balance its budget, and increase the competition power of export goods (devaluation) and did not provide the expected loan (Cosar, 2005). In 1960, the DP had to make a devaluation which was not held on the date indicated.

The most striking feature of this period is that sensitive principles on balanced budget and foreign borrowing, the building blocks of economic policies in the first years of the Republic, were abandoned and the main sources of development were determined as external debt and foreign capital. Therefore, in 1954, the Incentive Law was issued with extensive incentives and full freedom for profit and principle transfer to foreign capital.

GNP, which was 45.8 million TL in 1950 with respect to 1990 fixed prices, increased to 83.8 million TL in 1960 and annual average compound growth rate was 6.2%. In the same period, annual average inflation rate was 10.3% (Table 5-12).

Table 5-12 Main Macro Economic Figures in Period 1951-1960 (SSI, 2001, Pakdemirli, 2003)

Years	GNP (Million TL-1990 Constant)	GNP (Million USD)	GNP Increase (%-1990 Constant)	USD FX Increase (% Real)	Inflation (CPI %-December)
1951	51.78	6,058.84	13.12	-5.83	6.19
1952	58.96	6,966.81	13.88	-0.96	0.97
1953	66.80	8,120.95	13.30	-2.80	2.88
1954	61.77	8,280.74	-7.54	-9.32	10.28
1955	68.94	9,947.29	11.61	-7.09	7.63
1956	68.23	11,471.64	-1.04	-14.19	16.54
1957	76.71	15,250.72	12.43	-15.43	18.24
1958	79.35	18,211.38	3.45	-13.37	15.43
1959	82.65	22,722.67	4.15	-16.53	19.80
1960	83.81	7,553.99	1.41	205.04	5.37

When the budget figures in this period are analysed, it is noted that the budget deficit gained continuity and for the first time Turkey began to have budget deficits continuously. For this period, the average budget deficit was 46.8 million USD and the budget had deficits throughout the whole period (Table 5-13).

Table 5-13 Macro Economic Figures Related to Budget in Period 1951-1960 (SSI, 2001, Pakdemirli, 2003)

Years	Budget Deficit (Million USD)	Budget Deficit / Total Budget Revenue	Total Revenue (Million USD)	Total Expenses (Million USD)
1951	19.81	3.37	587.86	568.04
1952	-4.67	-0.58	798.51	803.18
1953	-7.83	-0.96	811.48	819.31
1954	-62.12	-7.28	853.85	915.98
1955	-57.32	-5.10	1,124.42	1,181.74
1956	-65.12	-5.52	1,180.30	1,245.42
1957	-70.05	-4.95	1,416.64	1,486.70
1958	-55.35	-3.21	1,722.17	1,777.52
1959	-122.21	-5.36	2,280.66	2,402.87
1960	-43.00	-5.58	770.36	813.37

Table 5-14 Macro Economic Figures Related to Indebtedness in Period 1951-1960 (SSI, 2001, Pakdemirli, 2003)

Years	Total Debt (Million USD)	Domestic Debt (Million USD)	External Debt (Million USD)	Total Debt/ GNP
1951	982.29	714.29	268.00	16.21
1952	1,044.00	750.00	294.00	14.99
1953	1,090.43	821.43	269.00	13.43
1954	1,161.14	857.14	304.00	14.02
1955	1,274.57	928.57	346.00	12.81
1956	1,384.29	964.29	420.00	12.07
1957	1,572.86	1142.86	430.00	10.31
1958	1,711.71	1285.71	426.00	9.40
1959	1,774.71	1285.71	489.00	7.81
1960	1,035.78	477.78	558.00	13.71

During the same period Turkey's debts increased; the external debt in 1950 with 277 million USD reached 558 million USD in 1960; and domestic debt increased 2.5 fold in the same period. The rapid fall observed in the domestic debts in 1960 occurred due to the devaluation and the decrease of the USD counterpart of domestic debt (Table 5-14).

The effects of abandoning the economic policies of the first years of the Republic and transitioning to a foreign source dependent growth model in the DP period are clearly seen in the data on foreign trade. Foreign trade (generally had a surplus in the previous period - World War II and the earlier period), had a deficit throughout this period (Table 5-15). The average annual trade deficit was 123.1 million USD and the export coverage rate of imports was realised to be 73.5%. The current account data obtained from this period onwards also had deficits and the annual average value was 129.7 million USD.

Table 5-15 Macro Economic Figures Related to Foreign Trade in Period 1939-1950 (SSI, 2001, Pakdemirli, 2003)

Years	Current Account Deficit/ GNP	Foreign Trade Deficit/ GNP	Foreign Trade Deficit (Million USD)	Current Account Deficit (Million USD)	Import (Million USD)	Export (Million USD)
1951	-1.6	-1.5	-88.00	-94.00	402.09	314.08
1952	-2.8	-2.8	-193.01	-198.00	555.92	362.91
1953	-2.0	-1.7	-136.47	-164.00	532.53	396.06
1954	-2.1	-1.7	-143.44	-177.00	478.36	334.92
1955	-1.8	-1.9	-184.29	-177.00	497.64	313.35
1956	-0.7	-0.9	-102.35	-75.00	407.34	304.99
1957	-0.4	-0.3	-51.91	-64.00	397.13	345.22
1958	-0.4	-0.4	-67.83	-64.00	315.10	247.27
1959	-0.6	-0.5	-116.18	-145.00	469.98	353.80
1960	-1.8	-2.0	-147.46	-139.00	468.19	320.73

In this period, it is noted that unlike period 1946-1950, vulnerabilities started to form, new policies were institutionalised and executives acted in line with these principles (the adoption of the free trade doctrine, the relaxing of protective measures) in terms of economic policies. However, this policy change became the reason for Turkey experiencing internal economic crises not experienced up to that date, except for the economic developments in the world (the 1929 World Economic Depression, 1939-1945 World War II). As a matter of fact, this development is just an ordinary example illustrating that after World War II, fostering the liberalisation of foreign trade in underdeveloped countries caused payment balance problems within a short period of time (Schmitz, 1996, p. 257).

Planned Economy Period (1960-1980)

After the DP was dismissed from the government by a military coup on the 27th of May 1960, firstly a transition government was formed, and after 1964 the Justice Party (JP), the successor of the DP came to power. After 1971, Turkey went through various political turbulences and it was governed by coalition governments until 1980. One of the important developments of this period was that after the years passing by without a plan, planning was emphasised and the SPO was established on the 30th of September 1960.

Another important development is that, in order to solve the problems arising from balance of payments, such import substitution policies as customs tariffs, quotas and rigid foreign exchange rate policies were chosen. Industrial investments became attractive with implementation characterised as random protectionism, starting with restrictive measures towards foreign trade. Those trading goods previously started to produce goods at home. From this perspective, the private sector leaned towards nondurable consumer goods; however, the public sector supported the SOEs which would produce both the consumer and intermediate goods (Cosar, 2005). Despite this, the private sector made investments in the form of the assembly industry in general.

In this period, GNP, with 1990 fixed prices increased from 83.8 million TL in 1960 to 241.9 million TL in 1980 and the annual average compound growth rate was 5.4%. In the same period, average annual inflation was realised as 19.8%. While the inflation on average was 5.17% before 1970, with the negative effect of the oil crisis after 1970, it rapidly increased and reached 93.8% in 1980 and average inflation between 1970 and 1980 was 34.4 % (Table 5-16).

When one looks at the budget figures in this period, it is seen that after transitioning to a planned economy, budget deficits decreased until 1967 and there were years when the budget even had a surplus, however later on, with the effect of the oil crisis in the 1970s, the budget deficit rapidly increased and the average budget deficit in this period was 459.5 million USD (Table 5-17).

Table 5-16 Main Macro Economic Figures in Period 1961-1980 (SSI, 2001, Pakdemirli, 2003)

Years	GNP (Million TL- 1990 Constant)	GNP (Million USD)	GNP Increase (%-1990 Constant)	USD FX Increase (% Real)	Inflation (CPI %- December)
1961	86.59	8,018.78	3.32	-2.67	2.75
1962	95.22	9,323.07	9.97	-5.42	5.73
1963	105.86	10,813.77	11.17	-4.15	4.33
1964	111.67	11,544.07	5.49	-1.19	1.20
1965	111.14	12,420.41	-0.47	-7.50	8.10
1966	126.31	14,798.85	13.64	-4.62	4.84
1967	130.32	16,427.62	3.18	-7.05	7.59
1968	140.04	18,210.30	7.46	-3.06	3.16
1969	146.11	20,372.91	4.34	-6.74	7.23
1970	155.15	13,994.26	6.18	54.58	6.74
1971	168.13	18,648.04	8.37	-18.67	15.92
1972	171.45	22,438.54	1.97	-15.25	18.00
1973	180.80	28,506.33	5.45	-16.99	20.47
1974	187.57	38,821.49	3.75	-23.82	29.86
1975	218.97	46,060.05	16.74	-1.61	10.07
1976	238.08	52,610.05	8.73	-4.81	15.56
1977	244.97	57,572.50	2.89	-5.97	24.08
1978	238.46	65,838.74	-2.66	-14.88	52.57
1979	254.24	82,186.37	6.62	-14.59	63.92
1980	241.96	68,390.64	-4.83	14.37	93.71

Table 5-17 Macro Economic Figures Related to Budget in Period 1961-1980 (SSI, 2001, Pakdemirli, 2003)

Years	Budget Deficit (Million USD)	Budget Deficit / Total Budget Revenue	Total Revenue (Million USD)	Total Expenses (Million USD)
1961	-49.86	-4.10	1,214.9	1,264.7
1962	-11.15	-1.11	1,002.0	1,013.1
1963	0.57	0.04	1,303.4	1,302.8
1964	-68.16	-4.75	1,435.6	1,503.7
1965	64.68	3.86	1,674.4	1,609.8
1966	-3.36	-0.18	1,913.1	1,916.5
1967	-71.34	-3.27	2,182.9	2,254.2
1968	-136.12	-6.10	2,233.0	2,369.1
1969	-277.76	-10.92	2,543.0	2,820.8
1970	-74.20	-3.47	2,139.0	2,213.2
1971	-405.71	-13.99	2,899.3	3,305.0
1972	2.06	0.06	3,639.2	3,637.2
1973	-203.84	-4.65	4,388.1	4,592.0
1974	-303.33	-5.71	5,312.3	5,615.7
1975	-93.34	-1.24	7,521.9	7,615.2
1976	-261.34	-2.86	9,134.3	9,395.7
1977	-2,287.23	-22.44	10,190.7	12,478.0
1978	-963.93	-7.45	12,944.2	13,908.1
1979	-1,891.98	-12.15	15,576.9	17,468.9
1980	-2,153.73	-18.31	11,761.7	13,915.4

In this period, the debts of Turkey increased; external debt which was 558 million USD in 1960, due to increase in foreign trade and current account deficit, reached 15,734 million USD in 1980 and domestic debt increased 81 fold. The decrease observed in domestic debts in 1980 was formed by the decrease of the USD counterpart of domestic debt after the devaluation (Table 5-18). Total debt which was 1 billion USD as of 1960 reached 25 billion USD in 1980 and the Total Debts/GNP ratio reached 37%.

Table 5-18 Macro Economic Figures Related to Indebtedness in Period 1961-1980 (SSI, 2001, Pakdemirli, 2003)

Years	Total Debt (Million USD)	Domestic Debt (Million USD)	External Debt (Million USD)	Total Debt / GNP
1961	1,599.9	988.9	611.0	20
1962	1,854.2	1,122.2	732.0	20
1963	1,914.6	1,255.6	659.0	18
1964	2,167.1	1,311.1	856.0	19
1965	2,822.9	1,388.9	1,434.0	23
1966	3,363.7	1,766.7	1,597.0	23
1967	3,732.2	2,022.2	1,710.0	23
1968	4,160.8	2,277.8	1,883.0	23
1969	4,563.1	2,511.1	2,052.0	22
1970	3,973.8	1,676.8	2,297.0	28
1971	4,574.1	2,107.1	2,467.0	25
1972	4,924.1	2,357.1	2,567.0	22
1973	5,664.0	2,750.0	2,914.0	20
1974	6,254.7	3,104.7	3,150.0	16
1975	7,650.0	4,400.0	3,250.0	17
1976	9,915.8	5,878.8	4,037.0	19
1977	11,570.0	6,961.0	4,609.0	20
1978	13,451.0	7,160.0	6,291.0	20
1979	26,091.1	11,857.1	14,234.0	32
1980	25,032.4	9,298.4	15,734.0	37

Table 5-19 Macro Economic Figures Related to Foreign Trade in Period 1961-1980 (SSI, 2001, Pakdemirli, 2003)

Years	Current Account Deficit/ GNP	Foreign Trade Deficit/ GNP	Foreign Trade Deficit (Million USD)	Current Account Deficit (Million USD)	Import (Million USD)	Export (Million USD)
1961	-2.1	-2.0	-160.5	-170	507.2	346.7
1962	-2.6	-2.6	-238.3	-242	619.4	381.2
1963	-2.8	-3.0	-319.5	-300	687.6	368.1
1964	-0.9	-1.1	-126.5	-109	537.2	410.8
1965	-0.6	-0.9	-108.2	-78	572.0	463.7
1966	-1.1	-1.5	-227.8	-164	718.3	490.5
1967	-0.7	-1.0	-162.3	-115	684.7	522.3
1968	-1.2	-1.5	-267.2	-224	763.7	496.4
1969	-1.1	-1.3	-264.4	-220	801.2	536.8
1970	-1.2	-2.6	-359.1	-171	947.6	588.5
1971	-0.6	-2.7	-494.2	-109	1,170.8	676.6
1972	0.0	-3.0	-677.6	-8	1,562.5	885.0
1973	1.7	-2.7	-769.1	484	2,086.2	1,317.1
1974	-1.9	-5.8	-2,245.3	-719	3,777.5	1,532.2
1975	-3.6	-7.2	-3,337.5	-1,648	4,738.6	1,401.1
1976	-3.9	-6.0	-3,168.4	-2,029	5,128.6	1,960.2
1977	-5.5	-7.0	-4,043.3	-3,140	5,796.3	1,753.0
1978	-1.9	-3.5	-2,310.9	-1,265	4,599.0	2,288.2
1979	-1.7	-3.4	-2,808.2	-1,413	5,069.4	2,261.2
1980	-5.0	-7.3	-4,999.2	-3,408	7,909.4	2,910.1

The fact is that the economic model, called import substitution could not actually turn into import preventive investments, and increasing oil prices gradually increased the external debt, and the foreign source dependent economic growth in the previous period created its own crisis. In this period, the dependency of import substitution private sector investments in Turkey on raw materials and intermediate goods from abroad prevented trade and the current account deficit from becoming positive in the same period. Despite this, local contribution prevented further growth in trade and current account deficit. Furthermore, Turkish workers starting to work abroad and foreign currencies from them had a positive effect on the current account deficit, and they even resulted in current account deficit become positive in 1973. However, sudden increases in oil prices in the same years increased the current account and trade deficits of Turkey, dependent on overseas countries in energy perspective (Table 5-19). The most important development observed in those years was that trade and current account deficits began to differentiate. As mentioned previously, the most important reason is the foreign currencies brought in by the workers abroad and companies in the construction business doing projects abroad. When improvement in the trade deficit in this period is reviewed, it is observed that the annual average trade deficit was 1.3 billion USD and current account deficit was 0.75 billion USD. While the trade deficit was 223 million USD on average until the 1970s, the oil crisis after 1970 increased the trade deficit and caused an increase to the level of 2.5 billion USD on average annually. The same progress is observed in the export coverage rate of imports and for this period export/import ratio was 56.3%.

After 1960, it is noted that despite implementing the planned economy model and the adoption of an import substitution system, economic indicators became much worse. While the first 10 years in the period 1960-1970 had relatively better indicators, indicators of the following 10 years between 1971 and 1980 became much worse. When assessing whether the indicators of the first 10 years were better or not, the effect of the devaluation at the beginning of the period should also be taken into account. Economic crisis, an inevitable result for economies which are not based on internal dynamics and are externally dependent, occurred in Turkey again in 1980 and with the economic decisions taken on the 24th of January 1980, capital provided through the liberty and import substitution model was abandoned.

CHAPTER SIX

COMPARING THE ECONOMIC POLICIES OF THE TURKISH REPUBLIC FROM THE PERSPECTIVE OF ECONOMIC DATA

When all the periods are analysed in terms of implemented economic policies, it is noted that until the 1950s, balanced budget and foreign trade surplus were adopted as the most important principles, and foreign borrowing and the emission of money (printing money without counterpart) were avoided. Keeping expenses in revenues in parallel, and borrowing only for investments considering pay back, were the main principles. A comparison of periods from the perspective of macro-economic figures crucial for the projected model as well as for general terms allows a comparison of the results of the policies implemented.

From a growth point of view, the periods when the GNP grew the most were the periods 1923-1929 and 1946-1950. For both of the periods, the annual compound average growth rate was 10.3% (Figure 6-1). These periods were post-war periods, and growths were in the form of the recovery of the economy that had downsized during the war. With an annual compound average growth rate of 7.0%, the period 1929-1938 had the highest growth rate.

When the export coverage rates of imports for the same periods are analysed, it is observed that the period 1938-1946 had the highest rate with 136.5%, and the period 1929-1938 had the second highest with 102.4% (Figure 6-2). Turkey, whose sovereignty authorities were restricted because of the Lausanne Agreement between 1923 and 1929, had a trade deficit and with the increase of customs and imports decreasing the industrialisation movement after 1929, a trade balance surplus was observed. This policy continued until 1947, after which the country had a trade deficit again with a more liberalised foreign trade policy. Starting from 1947 onwards, Turkey could not have a trade surplus anymore.

Figure 6-1 Annual Average GNP Increase of Turkey (SSI, 2001, Pakdemirli, 2003, Treasury, 2008a, TurkStat, 2008a)

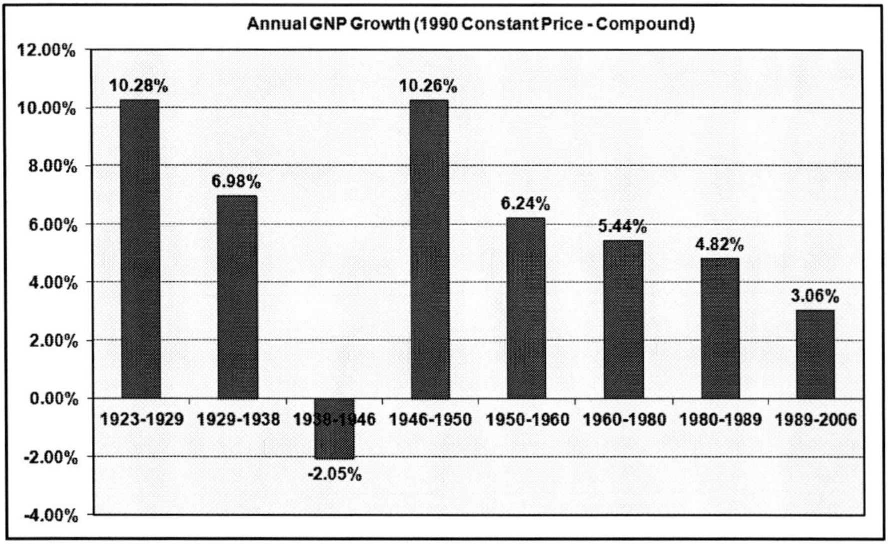

Figure 6-2 Annual Average Export Coverage Ratios of Imports of Turkey (SSI, 2001, Pakdemirli, 2003, Treasury, 2008b, TurkStat, 2008b)

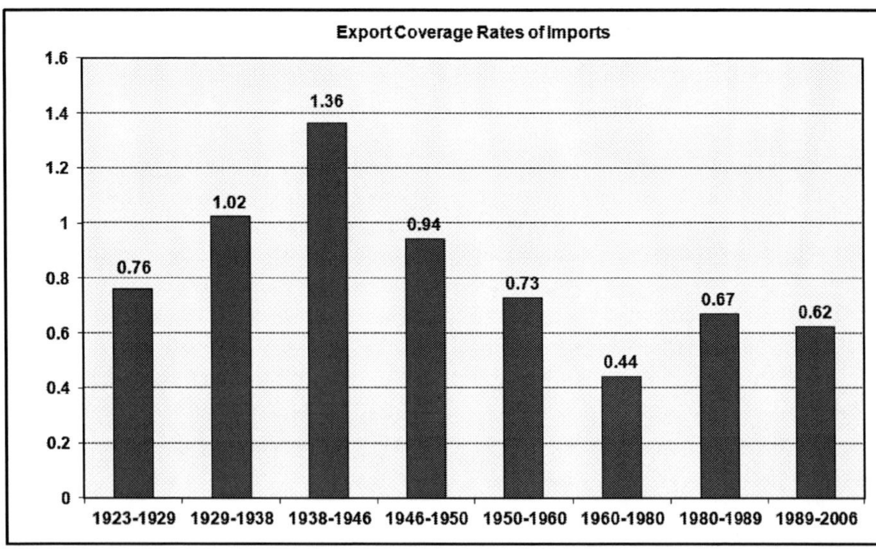

When the ratio of trade deficit to GNP is observed, the period 1938-1946 was the best period with 0.6%, and the period 1929-1938 was the second best period with a 0.1% surplus rate. In all other periods except two, it is observed that Turkey had continuous trade deficits. The trade deficit/GNP ratio, which progressively increased from 1950, was -9.8% for the period 1989-2006 (Figure 6-3).

Figure 6-3 Annual Average Foreign Trade Deficit/GNP Ratio of Turkey (SSI, 2001, Pakdemirli, 2003, Treasury, 2008a, 2008b, TurkStat, 2008a, TurkStat, 2008b)

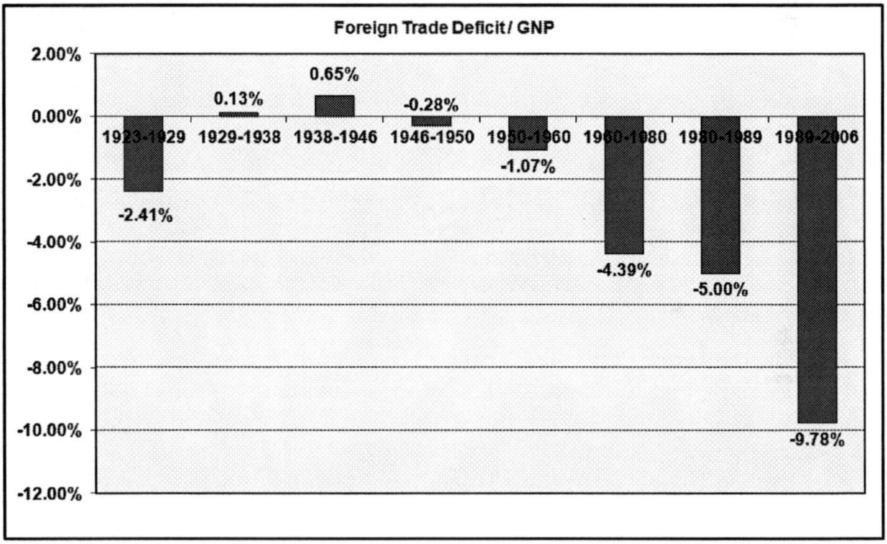

When analysed in terms of external debts, excluding the period 1923-1929, it was in 1929-1938 with the lowest External Debt/GNP ratio of 4.9%. 75 million TL debt inherited from the Ottoman Empire and actual payments were completed in 1944 according to the agreement in 1933 and were deducted in the calculations, and the effect of foreign borrowing in the period is shown (Figure 6-4). It is noted that after 1950, the External Debt/GNP ratio gradually increased and reached 51.4% in the period 1989-2006.

Figure 6-4 Annual Average External Debt/GNP Ratio of Turkey (Excluding Remaining Ottoman Empire Debts) (Cosar, 1996c, SSI, 2001, Pakdemirli, 2003, Treasury, 2008a, 2008c, 2008d, 2008f, Ozdemir, 2009b, TurkStat,2008a, TurkStat, 2008b)

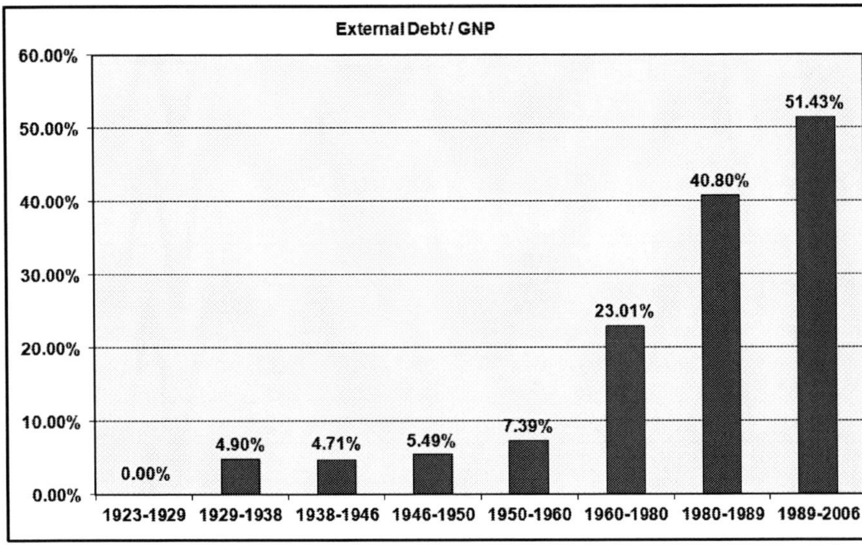

When the same periods are analysed in terms of budget, it is noted that Turkey had a budget surplus until the 1950s, but after the budget deficit it had in 1952, it did not have a budget surplus except for in 1963, 1965 and 1972.

When we look at growth and other economic indicators, it is observed that the period 1947-1950 was a period of significant changes in Turkey. In terms of full independence and the general strategy of the economy in the first years of the Republic, an externally dependent structure and foreign borrowing were avoided, but due to the developments in world politics after World War II and the desire to rank among the Western Bloc against the USSR threat, it was abandoned. In 1947, foreign trade and in the 1950s, the budget and a change in external debt policies, became prominent. Particularly changing economic strategies after 1950 provided Turkey with economic growth, albeit not as great as in previous periods; however the costs of this were trade, current account and budget deficits, increased indebtedness and an economic structure that was dependent on capital which would come from outside the country. Because of its structural defects, the externally dependent economy was the reason for continuously emerging crises and for the economic stability factor being wiped out.

Figure 6-5 Annual Average Budget Deficit or Surplus/Total Revenues Ratio of Turkey (SSI, 2001, Pakdemirli, 2003, Treasury, 2008a, 2008e)

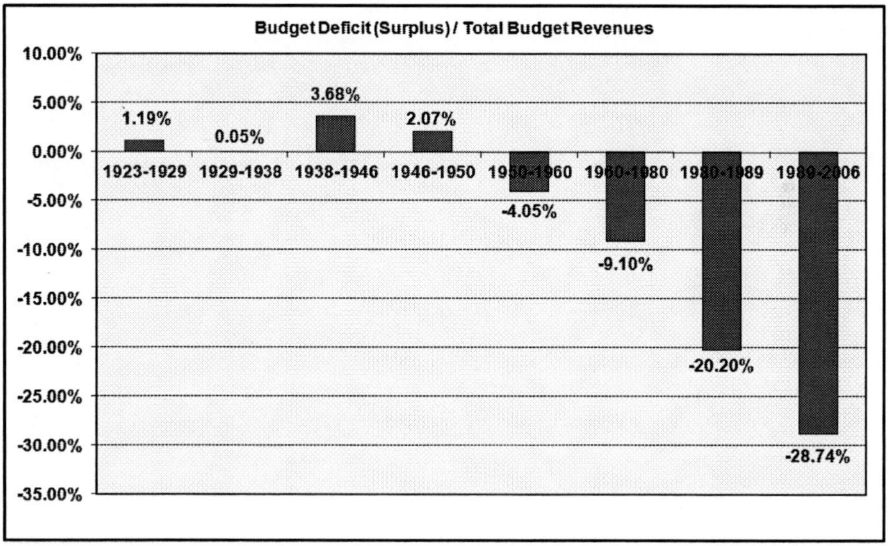

CHAPTER SEVEN

A MODEL FOR ASSESSING THE MACRO-ECONOMIC DATA OF IMPLEMENTED ECONOMIC MODELS FROM THE PERSPECTIVE OF ECONOMIC DEPENDENCY

In the study, an economic model defined between crisis and macro-economic variables with a multiple regression model was developed. In the variables used in the regression model, the Factor Analysis method was employed and variables that are many in number were gathered under certain groups. The model and variable determination work was conducted using the data from 1980-2008 and the model which was developed based on these data was applied for the pre-1980 period as well. Because some data could not be reached as we moved towards the years before 1980, in the periods where no data was available, a model based on the powerful variable was applied.

In this study, the main assumptions were the insufficient energy resources of oil and natural gas in Turkey, undeveloped industry in the first years of the Republic, absence of a national bourgeoisie, and extreme borrowing, all having two main consequences, namely dependency and crisis. Additionally, it was projected that the factor creating dependency was fear of crisis; it was the implementation of the policies increasing dependency in order not to be drawn into a crisis, and dependency was at peak level in years of crisis. At the beginning of the study, crisis years were reflected as 1994 and 2001.

The macro-economic variables were determined during a detailed literature search and used in the study presented in Table 7-1. While some of these data are raw data, some others are made up of variables calculated from more than one set of raw data. The values between 1980-2008 obtained from the State Planning Organisation (SPO), the Turkish Statistical Institution (TurkStat), the Undersecretariat of the Treasury (UT), the Turkish Electricity Transmission Corporation (TETC) and the

Central Bank of Turkish Republic (CBTR) are presented in Appendix A, Appendix B and Appendix C.

Table 7-1 All Variables

VARIABLE NO	DETAIL
1	Real GDP Growth
2	Change in Real FX Rate
3	Foreign Trade Deficit/GDP
4	Current Account Deficit/GDP
5	Oil Imports/Current Account Deficit
6	Electricity Consumption/GDP (kWh/2008 USD)
7	Oil Prices (2008 USD/Barrel)
8	Export Coverage Ratios of Imports
9	Capacity Utilisation Rate of Manufacturing Industry
10	Direct Tax/Total Tax
11	Total Budget Revenues/Total Budget Expenses
12	Total Debt/GDP
13	PSBR (Public Sector Borrowing Requirement)/GDP
14	M2/GDP
15	Domestic Loan/GDP
16	Budget Deficit/GDP
17	Foreign Currency Reserves/Import
18	External Debt/Foreign Currency Reserves
19	Industrial Production Index (1997=100)
20	Private Sector Debt/GDP
21	Unemployment Rate
22	Real Domestic Debt Interest (% TL)
23	Short Term Capital Movement/GDP
24	External Debt Principal Payment + Import/(Export+Foreign Currency Reserves)
25	Short Term Capital Movement/Foreign Currency Reserves
26	Treasury Bills USD Yield
27	Loss and Thief Ratio in Electricity
28	External Debt/GDP
29	Intermediate Goods Import/GDP

By applying Factor Analysis on the variables, the possibility of reaching a complement of more meaningful factors was researched.

Firstly, out of the determined variables, the variable numbered 29, which is Intermediate Goods Imports/GNP, could not be calculated for the period before 2000 due to being unable to obtain intermediate goods import data for that period; it was therefore excluded from the calculations. In addition, a correlation matrix between the calculated variables and calculations between variables were observed as well. Those variables having high correlations between them (>90%) were excluded. As a result of this, 8 variables mentioned in Table 7-2 were excluded from the calculations.

Table 7-2 Variables Excluded due to High Correlation

VARIABLE NO	DETAIL
6	Electricity Consumption/GDP (kWh/2008 USD)
10	Direct Tax/Total Tax
12	Total Debt/GDP
17	Foreign Currency Reserves/Import
18	External Debt/Foreign Currency Reserves
19	Industrial Production Index (1997=100)
22	Real Domestic Debt Interest (% TL)
26	Treasury Bills USD Yield

Furthermore, variances of variables, their progress between 1980 and 2008, and their reactions in the crisis years of 1994 and 2001 were analysed by identifying the variables whose variances were low (<0.1%) and whose crisis period developments did not consist of a change, and they were excluded from the calculations. As a result of this, 8 variables mentioned in Table 7-3 were excluded from the calculations.

For the remaining 12 variables presented in Table 7-4, Factor Analysis was used.

After Factor Analysis, the number of significant basic components with respect to the Kaiser criterion was determined to be 4. Basic components are the ones whose Eigen values are higher than 1. Twelve variables were gathered under 4 factors and it was determined that with these 4 factors 85% of total variance can be explained (Table 7-5).

Table 7-3 Variables Excluded Due to Low Variance

VARIABLE NO	DETAIL
7	Oil Prices (2008 USD/Barrel)
11	Total Budget Revenues/Total Budget Expenses
13	PSBR (Public Sector Borrowing Requirement)/GDP
14	M2/GDP
15	Domestic Loan/GDP
16	Budget Deficit/GDP
21	Unemployment Rate
27	Loss and Thief Ratio in Electricity

Table 7-4 Variables Used in the Study

VARIABLE NO	DETAIL
1	Real GDP Growth
2	Change in Real FX Rate
3	Foreign Trade Deficit/GDP
4	Current Account Deficit/GDP
5	Oil Imports/Current Account Deficit
8	Export Coverage Ratios of Imports
9	Capacity Utilisation Rate of Manufacturing Industry
20	Private Sector Debt/GDP
23	Short Term Capital Movement/GDP
24	External Debt Principal Payment + Import/(Export+Foreign Currency Reserves)
25	Short Term Capital Movement/Foreign Currency Reserves
28	External Debt/GDP

Table 7-5 Outputs of Factor Analysis (Eigen Values and Percentage of Total Variance Explained)

Component	Initial Eigen Values	Percentage of Total Variance Explained	Cumulative Percentage	Rotation Sums of Squared Loadings	Percentage of Total Variance Explained	Cumulative Percentage
1	**3.7808**	**31.507**	**31.507**	**3.3675**	**28.062**	**28.062**
2	**3.5919**	**29.933**	**61.440**	**2.9022**	**24.185**	**52.247**
3	**1.6434**	**13.695**	**75.135**	**2.2088**	**18.407**	**70.654**
4	**1.1833**	**9.861**	**84.996**	**1.7211**	**14.342**	**84.996**
5	0.6157	5.131	90.127			
6	0.5108	4.257	94.384			
7	0.2504	2.087	96.471			
8	0.1778	1.481	97.952			
9	0.0993	0.828	98.780			
10	0.0789	0.658	99.438			
11	0.0413	0.344	99.782			
12	0.0262	0.218	100.000			

Distribution of variables under the factors is presented in Table 7-6. When the distribution of variables under the factors is taken into account, the variables forming the factors and envisioned headings are as follows:

FACTOR 1 (F1): Foreign Trade and Capital Movements

1. Trade Balance Deficit/GDP (D3)
2. Current Account Deficit/GDP (D4)
3. Export Coverage Rate of Imports (D8)
4. Short Term Capital Movements */GDP(D23)
5. Short Term Capital Movements */Foreign Currency Reserves (D25)

**Short Term Capital Movement is Foreign Capital Movement.*

FACTOR 2 (F2): External Debts and Production

1. Manufacturing Industry Capacity Utilisation Rate (D8)
2. Private Sector Debt(External)/GDP(D20)
3. External Debt/GDP (D28)

FACTOR 3 (F3): Real Net Wealth Transfer Abroad

1. Change in Real FX Rate (D2)
2. External Debt Payments+Imports/(Exports+Foreign Currency Reserves) (D24)

FACTOR 4 (F4): Energy Import and Economic Growth

1. Real GDP Growth (D1)
2. Oil Import/Current Account Deficit (D5)

Table 7-6 Rotated Component Matrix (Extraction Method: Principal Component Analysis, Rotation Method: Varimax with Kaiser Normalisation)

No	Variables	Factor 1	Factor 2	Factor 3	Factor 4
D1	Real GDP Growth				0.5655
D2	Change in Real FX Rate			0.8825	
D3	Foreign Trade Deficit/GDP	0.7399			
D4	Current Account Deficit/GDP	0.8639			
D5	Oil Imports/ Current Account Deficit				-0.9370
D8	Export Coverage Ratios of Imports	0.7994			
D9	Capacity Utilisation Rate of Manufacturing Industry		0.6245		
D20	Private Sector Debt /GDP		0.9303		
D23	Short Term Capital Movement/GDP	-0.8380			
D24	External Debt Principal Payment +Import/(Export+ Foreign Currency Reserves)			0.8217	
D25	Short Term Capital Movement/Foreign Currency Reserves	-0.4749			
D28	External Debt/GDP		0.9218		

When the change in factors between 1980 and 2008 is analysed, (Figure 7-1 and Figure 7-2), a change in the crisis years and pre-crisis differentiation is remarkable.

Figure 7-1 Change of Factor 1, 2 and 3 in Period 1980-2008

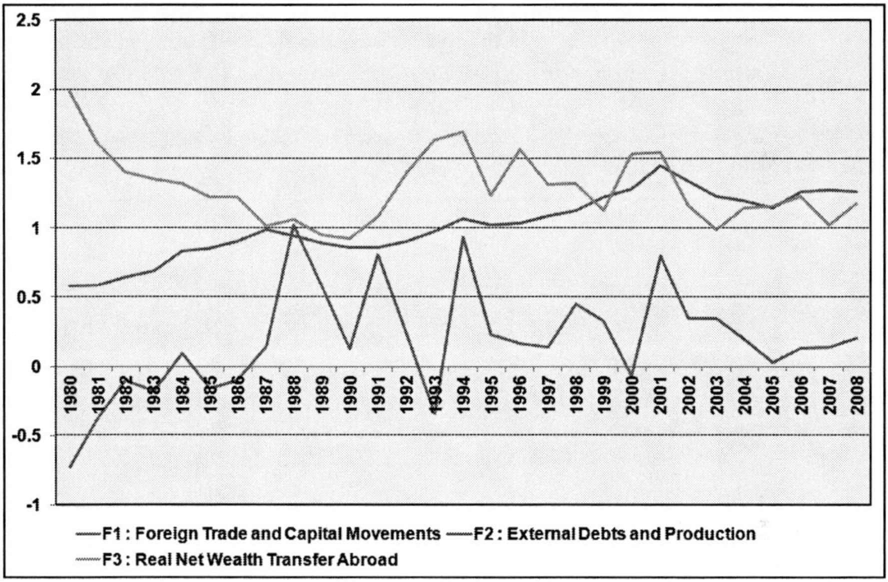

In addition to 1994 and 2001, differentiation was also observed in 1988, 1989, 1991 and 1998 as well. When these years are analysed we see that:

- **Year 1998:** Asian Crisis broke out.
- **Year 1991:** In 1991 events that would affect the economy of the country emerged. The most important of them are the Gulf Crisis and the collapse of the Union of Soviet Socialist Republics (USSR). In 1990, capital inflow of approximately 4 billion US Dollars (USD) increased the value of the Turkish Lira (TL), and valuation of TL caused a decline in exports and an increase in imports. In 1991 with the Gulf Crisis, decreasing tourism revenues due to capital outflow from Turkey (approximately 2.4 billion USD), Iraqi emigrants coming to Turkey and the war lured the

country into recession. All these developments led to an election on the 20th of October 1991.

- **Years 1988 and 1989:** The measures taken by the United States of America (USA) to settle the accumulated short term external debts resulted in a recession in the country; the collapse of the New York Stock Exchange in November 1987, wide-spread bankruptcies in the banking sector following this, the US economy entering into a long term recession, and the loss of value in the USD against strong currencies (like DM, Yen) created crises and this in turn had negative effects on the Turkish economy.

Figure 7-2 Change of Factor 4 in Period 1980-2008

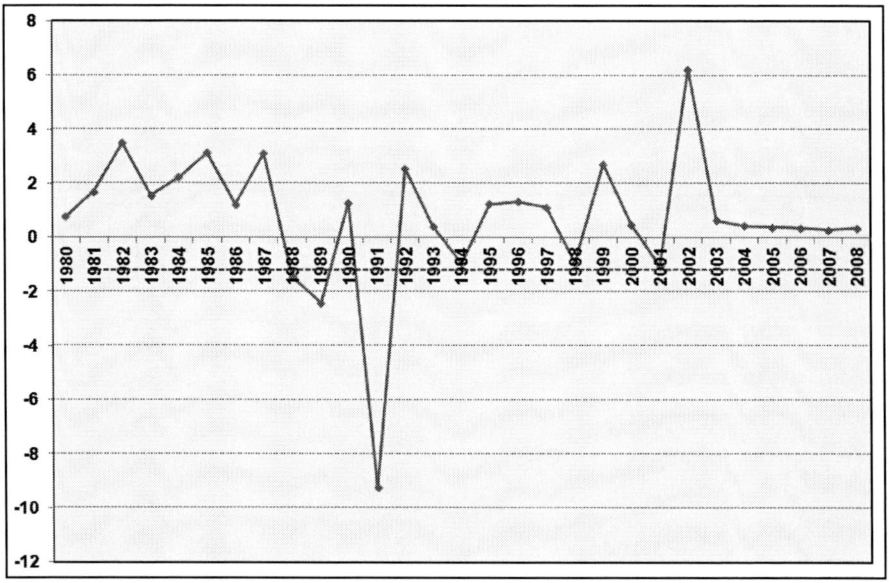

With the help of the coefficient presented in Table 3-9, obtained factors were calculated with respect to the years and presented in Table 7-7. Under the assumption that "As the Dependency Criterion, the crisis years have been projected as the highest indicator years", which is also one of the assumptions of the study, the years 1994 and 2001 were reflected as the highest indicator years from dependency perspective.

In other words, the years with the highest dependency were assumed to be 1994 and 2001. Under this assumption, calculations were made with crisis years to be 0 and normal years to be 1 in regression analysis.

Despite the fact that at the beginning of the study the crisis years were reflected as 1994 and 2001, due to the differentiation observed in 1988, 1989, 1991 and 1998 as well, the dependent variable was taken as 0 for these years and the results are presented in Table 7-8.

Table 7-7 Calculated Values of Factors in Period 1980-2008

Year	Factor 1	Factor 2	Factor 3	Factor 4
1980	-0.7264	0.5781	1.9859	0.7818
1981	-0.3735	0.5869	1.6141	1.6834
1982	-0.1006	0.6432	1.4043	3.5002
1983	-0.1780	0.6893	1.3529	1.5610
1984	0.0974	0.8358	1.3205	2.2286
1985	-0.1553	0.8512	1.2208	3.1324
1986	-0.0970	0.9015	1.2240	1.2206
1987	0.1489	0.9913	1.0122	3.1197
1988	1.0188	0.9446	1.0598	-1.4365
1989	0.5801	0.8939	0.9478	-2.4291
1990	0.1238	0.8563	0.9257	1.2915
1991	0.8060	0.8575	1.0797	-9.2414
1992	0.2333	0.9058	1.3956	2.5578
1993	-0.3430	0.9781	1.6357	0.4051
1994	0.9378	1.0641	1.6972	-0.9423
1995	0.2321	1.0220	1.2329	1.2374
1996	0.1637	1.0375	1.5660	1.3464
1997	0.1375	1.0832	1.3122	1.1235
1998	0.4539	1.1248	1.3175	-0.9383
1999	0.3299	1.2221	1.1219	2.7218
2000	-0.0647	1.2818	1.5336	0.4867
2001	0.7994	1.4501	1.5485	-1.0513
2002	0.3465	1.3416	1.1608	6.2314
2003	0.3464	1.2289	0.9908	0.6491
2004	0.1983	1.1936	1.1448	0.4489
2005	0.0306	1.1465	1.1592	0.3955
2006	0.1343	1.2615	1.2312	0.3576
2007	0.1417	1.2761	1.0223	0.3035
2008	0.2033	1.2640	1.1764	0.3635

Table 7-8 Statistical Values and Outputs of First Regression Analysis

Regression Statistics	**Values**
Multiple R	0.959766909
R^2	**0.921152519**
Adjusted R^2	0.852455717
Standard Error	0.264738833
F Significance	0.000000000
Number of Observations	22

Factor	**Coefficient**	**Standard Error**	**t Values**	**P Values**
F1	-0.752142129	0.211153596	3.562061661	0.002227412
F2	0.702929297	0.278556269	2.523473264	0.021244242
F3	**0.107117661**	**0.175027694**	**0.612004067**	**0.548188478**
F4	0.063372923	0.027026828	2.344815402	0.030703167

As seen in Table 7-8, although representation power of the relationship obtained is high (R^2 = 92.11%), the third factor F3, has not turned out to be statistically significant and its P value reached 0.54, which is much higher than the threshold value. Therefore, the 3rd factor F3 was excluded and the regression analysis was repeated and the results of the analysis are presented in Table 7-9.

It is observed that the representation power of the relation obtained as a result of the regression analysis made with the three factors is high (R^2 = 91.95%) and all the factors are statistically significant.

As a result of the analysis conducted, the crisis (dependency) could be stated as a statistically significant function of three factors included as independent variables. This function is called the Dependency Index (DI) and is stated as follows:

$$\mathbf{DI = -0.829*F1+0.867*F2+0.060*F4} \quad (1)$$

When the changes in the DI function between 1980 and 2008 are analysed, differentiation in crisis years is determined (Figure 7-3). As a result of the analysis on the obtained function, the crisis interval is observed as -0.60 and +0.60.

Table 7-9 Statistical Values and Outputs of Final Regression Analysis

Regression Statistics	Values
Multiple R	0.958911799
R^2	**0.919511839**
Adjusted R^2	0.858407822
Standard Error	0.260344971
F Significance	0.000000000
Number of Observations	22

Factor	Coefficient	Standard Error	t Values	P Values
F1	-0.828917883	0.167028631	4.962729307	0.00008640
F2	0.866924345	0.074822037	11.58648413	0.00000000
F4	0.059824299	0.025959388	2.304534199	0.03264770

Figure 7-3 Change of the DI Function in Period 1980-2008

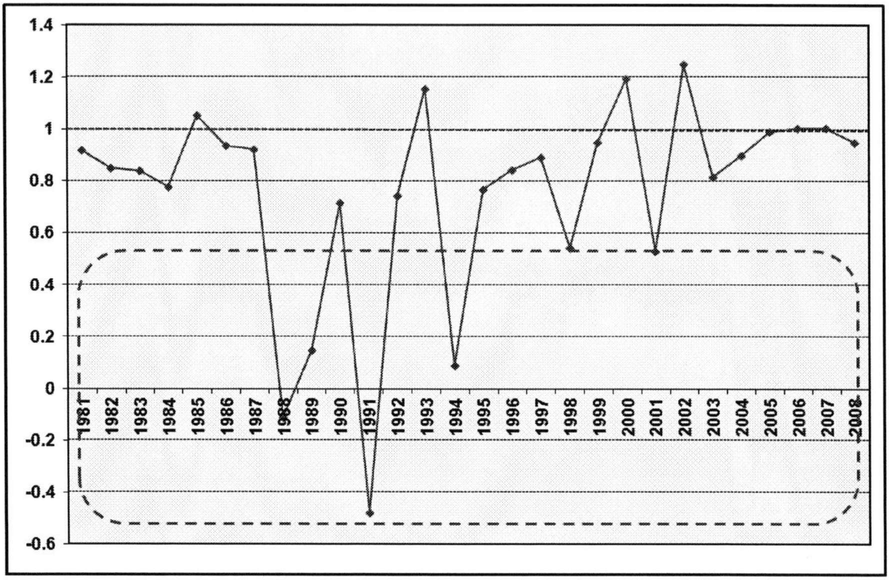

When one looks at the weights on factors in the calculation of the DI function between 1980 and 2008, they have the following weights:

Factor 1 : 20%,
Factor 2 : 71%,
Factor 4 : 9%.

When analysis is based on the Powerful Variable (PV) in each factor, in the calculation of each factor the variables with the most powerful multiplier were assessed as the PV and regression analysis was made again. The PVs defined in the factors in the DI function are presented in Table 7-10.

Table 7-10 Powerful Variables

Factor	PV	Variable No	Multiplier
F1 : Foreign Trade and Capital Movements	Current Account Deficit/GDP	D4	0.86393
F2 : External Debts and Production	External Debt/GDP	D28	0.92181
F4 : Energy Import and Economic Growth	Oil Import/Current Account Deficit	D5	-0.93700

With the PVs a regression analysis was made and a statistically defined result was obtained (Table 7-11). It is noted that the representation power of the relation obtained as a result of regression analysis with the three PVs is high (R^2 = 90.78%) and all the powerful variables are statistically significant.

As a result of the analysis, the DI could be stated as a statistically significant function where the determined three PVs are involved as independent variables. From the perspective of PVs, the DI is functionally defined as follows:

$$\mathbf{DI(PV) = -9.8821xPV1+0.9945xPV2-0.0906xPV4} \quad \mathbf{(2)}$$

When the change in DI(PV) function between 1980 and 2008 is analysed, as shown in Figure 7-4, the values below +0.45 turned out to be dependency (crisis) indicators.

PVs weights in DI(PV) were calculated and are presented in Table 7-12. As shown in the table, External Debt/GDP and Current Account Deficit/GDP ratios have a total effect of 96%.

Table 7-11 Statistical Values and Outputs of Regression Analysis with Powerful Variables

Regression Statistics	Values
Multiple R	0.952786882
R^2	**0.907802843**
Adjusted R^2	0.860427071
Standard Error	0.284839425
F Significance	28
Number of Observations	0.952786882

Factor	Coefficient	Standard Error	t Values	P Values
PV1	-9.882066149	1.876574141	-5.26601423	0.00001875
PV2	0.994524052	0.138299185	7.19110566	0.00000015
PV4	-0.090561183	0.019984746	4.53151533	0.00012551

Figure 7-4 Change of the DI(PV) Function in Period 1980-2008

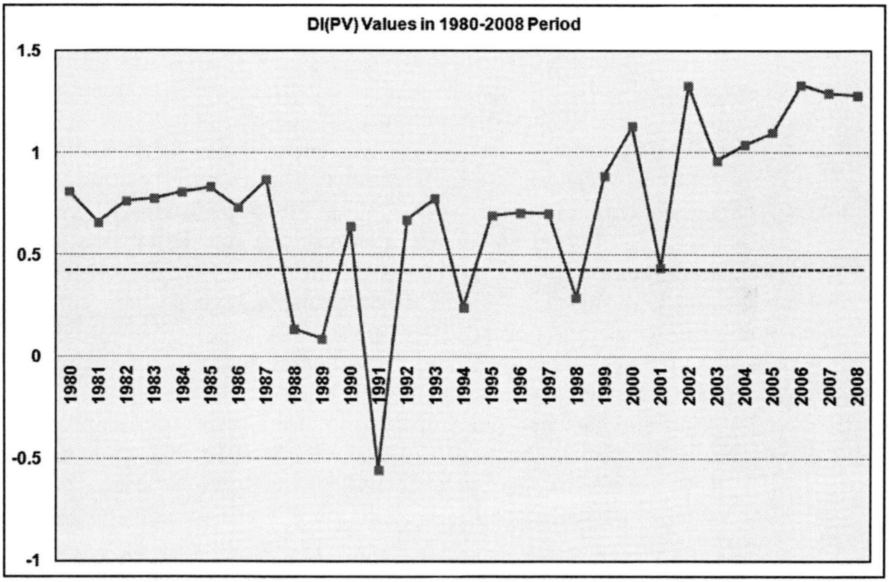

Table 7-12 Shares of PVs in DI(PV) Values in Period 1980-2008

PV	Detail	Share in DI(PV) %
PV1	Current Account Deficit/GDP	12
PV2	External Debt/GDP	84
PV4	Oil Import/Current Account Deficit	4

In the calculations under the assumption that dependency in times of crisis is at the highest level, which is the assumption of the study, DI(PV) is expected to be equal or close to 0 in times of crisis. Despite this, when the multipliers of DI(PV) are analysed, the multiplier of the Current Account Deficit/GDP ratio is -9.8821 and with the increasing current account deficit (in the calculations current account deficit had a negative sign), it will be a positive large number. The multiplier of the External Debt/GDP ratio however is 0.9945, and as a result of increasing external debt (in the calculations external debt had a positive sign), it will be an increasing positive number. It is clearly seen that the sum of the positive numbers, which are the result of these two negative elements, will be greater than 0 and close to 1. The worsening of these variables has a dependency increasing effect. In a crisis situation, which is the peak point of dependency, because of these rates worsening and becoming close to 1 and at least different from 0, and giving just the opposite result to the DI(PV) function, an important point is reflected. Due to such reasons as the current account deficit turning positive in times of crisis in Turkey, and the increasing energy import share in the current account deficit due to decrease in imports, in other words due to the decrease in the imports of intermediate and consumption goods, crisis years emerge as the years when equilibriums return to normal and reach the levels they should be at. It is observed that an economic structure based on current account deficit and growth with foreign sources in Turkey leads to the disruption of economic growth and balances again, and this in turn disrupts the balances and prepares a foundation for the formation of crisis. In this structure causing a growth-crisis vicious cycle, in order not to have a crisis, the current account deficit should be financed, in other words foreign sources should be secured.

CHAPTER EIGHT

EFFECT OF ECONOMIC VARIABLES ON ECONOMIC DEPENDENCE

The DI and DI(PV) functions[1] which are the Dependency Index functions determined for the 1980-2008 period mentioned in the previous chapter, very clearly set forth the differentiation in the crisis years. Because all of the variables necessary to determine the values of Factor 1, Factor 2 and Factor 4 which constitute the DI function in pre-1980 period could not be found, the DI(PV) function was used to compare the periods before 1980. The figures for the Current Account Deficit/GDP, External Debt/GDP variables which make up the DI(PV) function could be found until 1968, in previous years however, Current Account Deficit/GNP and External Debt/GNP ratios could be calculated. In Turkey, GNP and GDP are generally very close to each other and for 1968-2008 the GDP/GNP ratio was calculated as 99.1%. Therefore, the difference between GDP and GNP was regarded as being at a negligible level, and for the period before 1980 the Current Account Deficit/GNP and External Debt/GNP ratios were used. Despite the fact that the Current Account Deficit/GNP ratio was unavailable before 1950, because of such reasons as there being few capital movements for that period, there were no currency movements like tourism, contracting or workers' revenues, which emerged in the following periods and despite the fact that the arithmetic average of the difference between the current account and trade deficit was 5% in the 1950-1960 period, the difference between them was regarded as negligible and instead of the Current Account Deficit/GNP ratio, the Trade Deficit/GNP ratio was used. However, the Oil Imports/Current Account Deficit ratio could not be calculated for the pre-1980 period. Because in the calculations for the Period 1980-2008 arithmetic average of this ratio's weight in the total result was calculated as 4%, it was regarded as negligible, and with the other two variables calculations were made for the

[1] In this study, the Dependency Index was identified in two ways, as functions dependent on factors and variables; the DI function was identified as dependent on functions and the DI(PV) function was identified as dependent on variables.

period before 1980. As a result of this, for the pre-1980 period the DI(PV) was calculated by the below function:

DI(PV) =-9.8821xCurrent Account Deficit/GNP+0.9945xExternalDebt /GNP(3)

When the weights of the variables in the DI(PV) function are reviewed, the Current Account Deficit/GNP ratio was calculated to have a weight of 70% while the External Debts/GNP ratio was calculated to have a weight of 30%. The rates show that the current account deficit has a significant effect on dependency.

As can be seen from the DI(PV) function's values in 1923-1980, the period in which dependency was the lowest in terms of macro-economic values was the period of 1930-1946 (Figure 8-1). In the calculations performed by excluding the debts remaining from the Ottoman Empire it is noted that values for this period improved. Here the limit value was calculated to be approximately 0.07. It is observed that after 1946 these values could only be reached in crisis times in 1958, 1959, and 1973. While the DI(PV) value was kept at or under 0.07 through the economic policies applied until 1946, it has emerged that as a result of the decline of the economic structure after the applied polices following 1947—particularly 1950—the DI(PV) value could approach these values only in the crisis periods when balances are restored, but this restoration was short lived (Figure 8-1).

After 1980 the DI(PV) function was calculated to be roughly 0.44, and except for 1991 its average was calculated to be approximately 0.26 (Figure 7-4). It was projected that the Oil Imports/Current Account Deficit ratio, which was PV4 in the calculation of the DI(PV) value in 1991, had a weight of 71%, however for the calculations for all periods it had a weight of 4%; the DI(PV) function obtained with the exclusion of PV4 would provide a more appropriate comparison possibility with the pre-1980 period. Therefore, change in 1980-2008 of the DI(PV) function, which was formed by excluding PV4 is given in Figure 8-2.

Figure 8-1 DI(PV) Values in Period 1923-1980 Excluding PV4

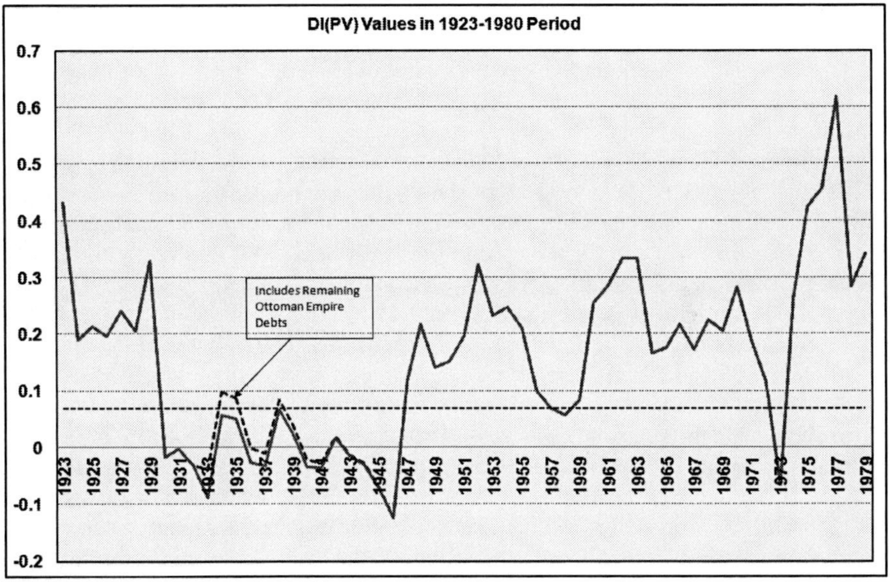

Figure 8-2 DI(PV) Values in Period 1980-2008 Excluding PV4

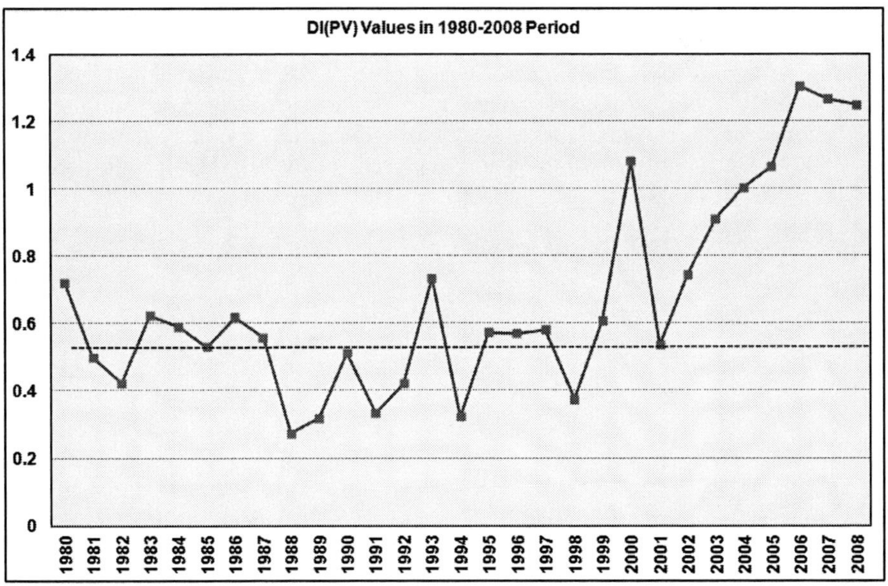

When the post-1980 values are analysed, while the average value was 0.53, the DI(PV) average in the crisis years was 0.36 (Figure 8-2). When the DI(PV) value's progress over the years is analysed, it is noted that Turkey was in a vicious cycle where once the economy started to grow, balances were disrupted again and as a crisis approached, balances were restored with a crisis. Despite this, it is observed that after 1980 the restorations attained in the crisis years were not at an adequate level and dependency gradually increased, as shown in Figure 8-3.

When the crisis years are observed, it is seen that after the adoption of free foreign trade, the DI(PV) value gradually increased and restorations taking place in crisis years were not at an adequate level. Despite this, as a result of policies applied during 1929-1946, the current account and external debt balance in the economy were formed. The policies of balance in foreign trade and sensitivity in foreign borrowing, which were abandoned after 1946, caused an economic structure where economic growth brought crisis and increased dependency. The reflection of an inability to have control over foreign trade, which was the result of the inability to have authority over customs before 1929, manifests itself with high DI(PV) values. Taking the necessary precautions on foreign trade or current account deficit upon the lifting of the validity of the Lausanne Agreement's articles restricting the authorities over customs, reflect that the policies followed were deliberate. The thought that full independence cannot be attained with an economic structure which drives towards a crisis through current account deficit and foreign borrowing, and whose dependency is high, emerged as an outcome of the negative experiences that the Republic's founding fathers went through in the Ottoman Empire. Because of the reasons mentioned, when the DI(PV) values in periods 1930-1938 and 1939-1946 were analysed in detail, the results are presented in Table 8-1.

Figure 8-3 DI(PV) Values in Crisis Years and in Period 1923-1947 Excluding PV4

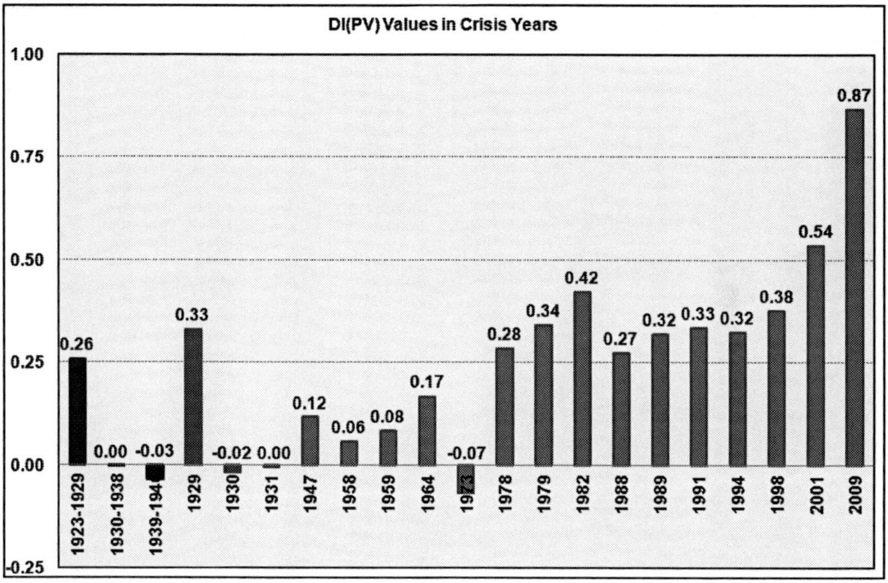

Table 8-1 Minimum, Maximum and Average DI(PV) Values in 1929-1946 Period

Period	Minimum DI(PV)	Maximum DI(PV)	Average DI(PV)
1930-1938	**-0.09**	**0.07**	**0.00**
1939-1946	-0.12	0.03	-0.03
1930-1946	**-0.12**	**0.07**	**-0.02**

CHAPTER NINE

RELATION LEVEL BETWEEN ECONOMIC AND POLITICAL DECISIONS WITH ECONOMIC DATA

It is noted that important decisions in Turkish political life coinciding generally with after-crisis times, is due to the obligations that the crisis brings along. After the 1958 crisis, as a result of the agreement signed with the IMF, devaluation was made and the stability package proposed by the IMF was put into effect. In 1964, Turkey calling off the intervention decision declared earlier upon the letter known as the Johnson Letter written against the possibility of Turkey using its guarantor rights regarding Cyprus and to prevent Turkey's operation in Cyprus, emerged as an important political event. Turkey, which evolved into a situation where it could not import anything other than its vital needs, signed an agreement again with the IMF in 1978 and made a devaluation, as a result of pressure from the World Bank and IMF, the decisions called "the 24th of January Decisions" were taken, and by putting the planned economy on the back burner, transitioned to a market economy, and upon the request of the USA, lifted its veto against Greece in NATO (Soyak and Eroglu, 2008, Kazgan, 2009).

After the 1988 crisis, such policies emerged as providing full liberty to capital by a change made to the Law on the Protection of Turkish Currency in 1989. After the 1994 crisis, other policies occurred, such as opposing other countries entering the Customs Union without benefiting from European Union harmonisation funds or a membership, accepting international arbitrage after the 1998 crisis, accepting application of the GATT in the most advanced way, opening up the financial institutions as well as all infrastructure institutions, sectors and SOEs to foreign capital after the 2001 crisis, the state's withdrawal from the economy, and accepting privatisation policies. In 2003, standing by the USA in the intervention in Iraq, an agreement was signed in order to get funds. Turkey and the USA signed the financing agreement which would provide Turkey with a loan of up to 8.5 billion USD on the 22nd of 2003 and it was planned that the loan should be used within 18 months and in 4 equal instalments. Within the framework of the financing agreement, each loan drawdown was contingent upon Turkey's meeting the conditions mentioned in the relevant US legislation, and the two conditions in question were stated as follows:

- Turkey carrying out a strong economic policy
- Turkey being in cooperation with the USA government regarding the Iraq issue

The crisis which Turkey used for its benefit seems to be the crisis in 1929. Following the 1929 crisis, and after the Lausanne Agreement articles restricting the authorities over customs lost their validity, Turkey brought its customs and foreign trade under control, began to implement a statist policy as the first country among the democratic countries in the world, while at the same time it made nationalisations in such services as water, railways and sea transportation, which were given to foreigners as concessions, and started to develop its own manufacturing industry (Kazgan, 2009). After the second half of the 1930s, some problems were encountered firstly with Italy due to the Eastern Mediterranean and Montreux Agreement and later with France over the Hatay issue, accordingly Italy was a side to the Montreux Agreement and Hatay on the other hand joined Turkey in 1939. During World War II, starting in 1939, both sides pressured Turkey to join the war on their side, but Turkey remained neutral throughout the war period.

The above mentioned developments occurred at the levels corresponding to DI(PV) values, which are presented in Figure 8-3. As explained in the previous chapter, as a result of changing economic policies following 1946, crises are correction times and the values corresponding to these dates are post-correction values. Therefore, when analysing the DI(PV) values after 1946, the DI(PV) values one year before the crisis are important due the fact that they show the level that the pre-crisis economy reached (Figure 9-1).

The DI(PV) values had been increasing before the crisis and it decreased again with the correction formed in the crisis. This structure shows the same characteristics as the crises taking place after economic growth stemming from changing economic policy following 1946 and restoration of economic balances (Figure 8-3 and Figure 9-1). Particularly after the 1970s, equilibrium DI(PV) value has been gradually increasing, this increase has been accelerating since the year 2000 and it is observed that the equilibrium point comes to 0.87.

Figure 9-1 DI(PV) Values before Crisis Years and in Period 1923-1946 Excluding PV4

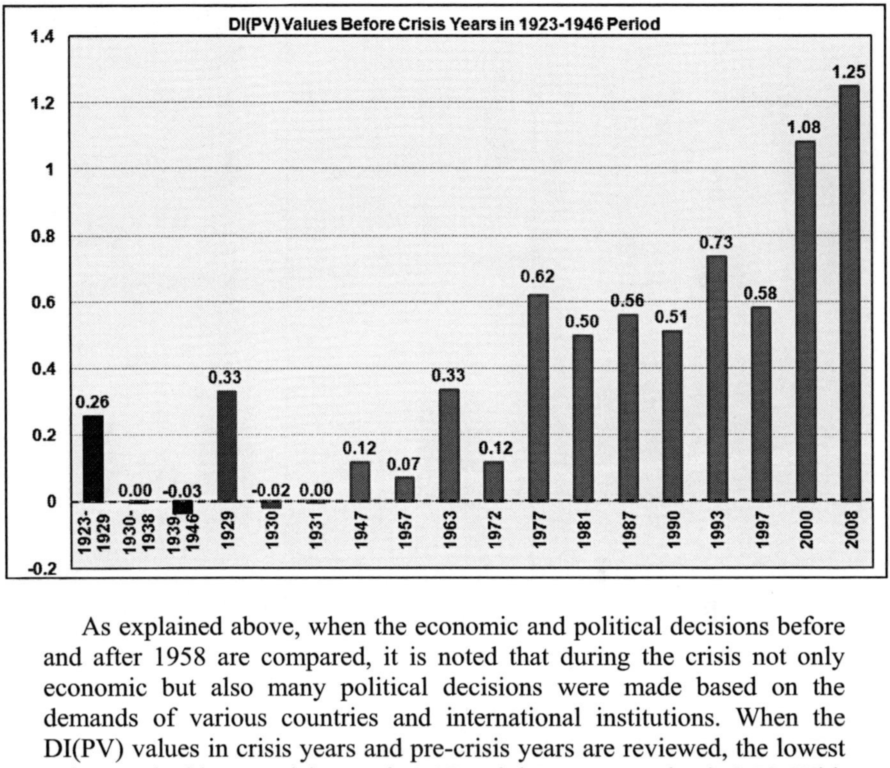

As explained above, when the economic and political decisions before and after 1958 are compared, it is noted that during the crisis not only economic but also many political decisions were made based on the demands of various countries and international institutions. When the DI(PV) values in crisis years and pre-crisis years are reviewed, the lowest value reached in pre-crisis year is 0.07 and the average value is 0.58. With the correction formed by the crisis, these values decreased to a lowest point of -0.07 and an average of 0.33 (Table 9-1). Particularly when the post-1980 period is analysed, the average pre-crisis DI(PV) value is 0.75, with the crisis it has dropped to an average of 0.45 and 0.27 as the lowest.

When the period before 1946 is analysed however, the maximum DI(PV) value is 0.07 and average DI(PV) value was -0.02 (Table 8-1). When compared to 0.58, which is the average of pre-1946 periods, this figure becomes important in understanding the differentiation between the decisions made before and after this date.

Table 9-1 Maximum, Minimum and Average DI(PV) Values before and in the Crisis Years

Crisis Periods	DI(PV) Values in Crisis Years	DI(PV) Values before Crisis Years
1958	0.06	0.07
1964	0.17	0.33
1973	-0.07	0.12
1978	0.28	0.62
1982	0.42	0.50
1988	0.27	0.56
1991	0.33	0.51
1994	0.32	0.73
1998	0.38	0.58
2001	0.54	1.08
2009	0.87	1.25
Minimum	**-0.07**	**0.07**
Maximum	**0.87**	**1.25**
Average	**0.33**	**0.58**

CHAPTER TEN

PROPOSED ECONOMIC MODEL WITHIN THE FRAMEWORK OF DEVELOPED MODEL

As explained in the previous chapter, the results of economic policies that were followed before 1946 were different to those after 1946 from the point of view of DI(PV). The obtained DI(PV) results allow for the determination of the limit values in terms of economic dependency (Table 10-1 and 10-2). In light of the findings, from the perspective of economic and political decisions for an economic dependency level that would allow acting independently and protecting its own interests, the DI(PV) value should be equal to or less than 0 and upper limit values should be 0.07 (Table 8-1). Another important point is that the DI(PV) value should have continuity at the determined levels. In the crises after 1958, the DI(PV) value was decreasing but it increased again just after a crisis. This situation arose from the structure of the economy. Over the determined limit value however, dependency gradually increased. Except for the crisis years in and after 1947 the DI(PV) value never dropped below 0.10 and in every crisis period, dependency increased and the DI(PV) value level increased (Figure 10-1).

In light of the assessments made, DI(PV) limit values from the point of view of Economic Dependence are presented in Figure 10-2. The determined limit values are of key importance in the economic model to be proposed. Accepting the DI(PV) value as 0 means that the total of the variables makes up the DI(PV) equals 0. When numerically stated, this is as follows:

0 = -9.8821xCurrent Deficit/GNP+0.9945xExternal Debt/GNP (4)

From this equation;

9.8821xCurrent Deficit/GNP= 0.9945xExternal Debt/GNP (5)

is found, and the result of this is given in the equations below:

External Debt = 9.936477782 x Current Deficit **(6)**
Current Deficit = 0.100639283 x External Debt **(7)**

In the calculations, if in the calculation of the Current Account Deficit/GNP ratio, the current deficit being negative and the current supply and the External Debt/GNP ratio being positive are taken into account, in order to satisfy this equation, the current account surplus must definitely be present. In this way, the External Debt amount that there can be for an acceptable economic dependency level is linked to the amount that can be paid by the current account surplus. In such a circumstance, the current account surplus emerges as a necessary condition and the External Debt level that can be paid by the current surplus emerges as a sufficient condition.

Figure 10-1 Average and Minimum Values of DI(PV) Except Crisis Years Excluding PV4

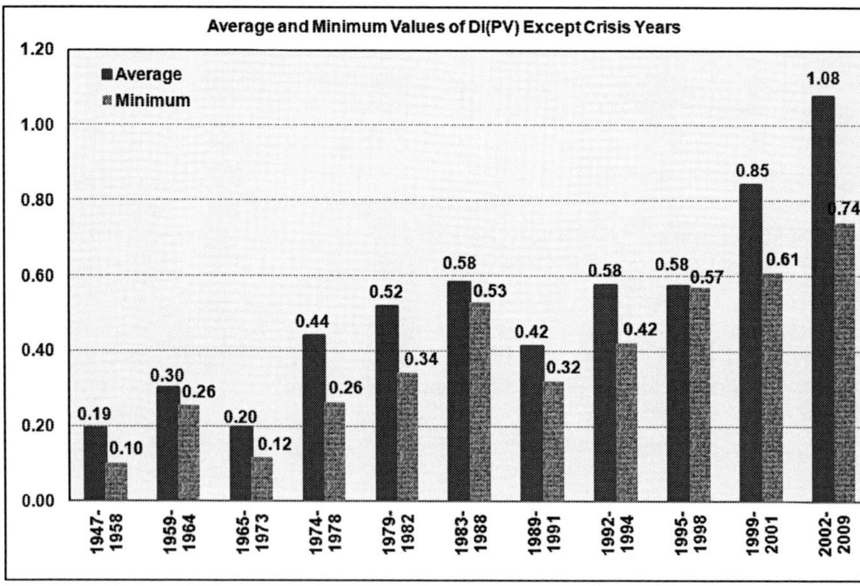

Figure 10-2 DI(PV) Limit Values Scheme in terms of Economic Dependency

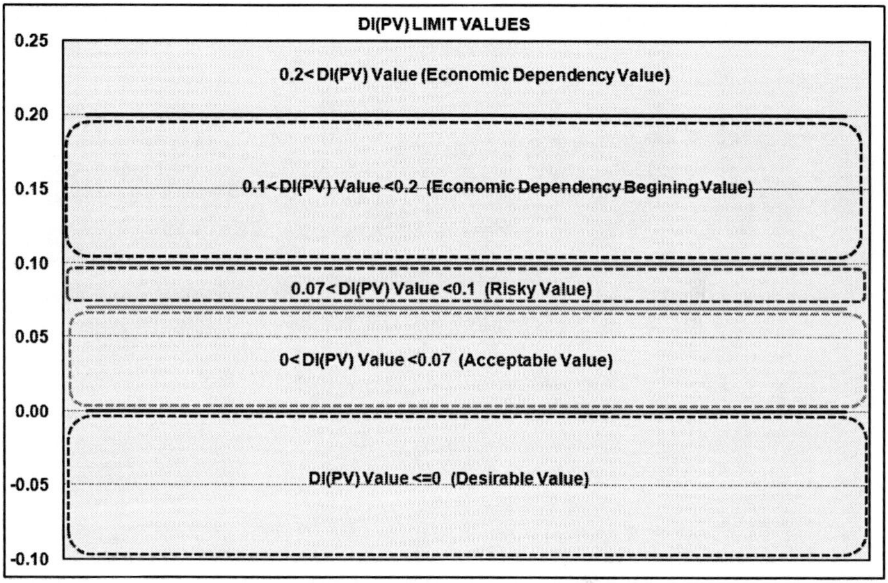

The DI(PV) value becoming greater than 0 can occur in two ways:

1. Having a current account deficit (because of a negative sign of current account deficit)
2. Having a high level of External Debt even when there is a current account surplus

In both of the above mentioned situations, because of an increasing dependency on sources that will come from outside, the economic dependency level will increase.

In light of the assessments made, for an economic dependency level that will allow it to protect its own interests in terms of economic and political decisions and to act independently, Turkey primarily should have a current account surplus. However this alone is not sufficient; between the current account surplus and Turkey's External Debt the equation stated in formula number 4 should be satisfied.

As of the year 2009, 0.87, which was calculated as the DI(PV) value of Turkey, is well above the limit values. Due to the fact that Turkey had had a current account deficit, it is clear that under all circumstances, the

DI(PV) values will be greater than 0. As of 2009, Turkey's total External Debt was 268.2 billion USD and the amount of current supply that should be present with respect to this debt amount and DI(PV) limit values is given in Figure 10-3. As can be seen from there too, Turkey should have a current account surplus in the range of 24-27 billion USD. However, the actual situation is approximately a 14 billion USD current account deficit. When the facts that 2009 was a crisis year, that this figure is a current account deficit figure found after correction in a contracting economy, and that in the previous year the current account deficit was 41 billion USD, are taken into account, the total correction that has to be made should be at least 41+24= 65 billion USD. This is possible through an increase in imports equal to this amount or a decrease in imports or the joint contribution of both. Generally speaking, for the products excluding the indispensable raw material imports like oil, a decrease in imports with a new industrialisation move that will increase the share of domestic production is possible by increasing the share in international markets, with production based on brand and innovation instead of making contract manufacturing, and by increasing the exports and provision of required corrections.

Figure 10-3 Required Current Account Surplus for Turkey in 2009 Regarding DI(PV) Limit Values

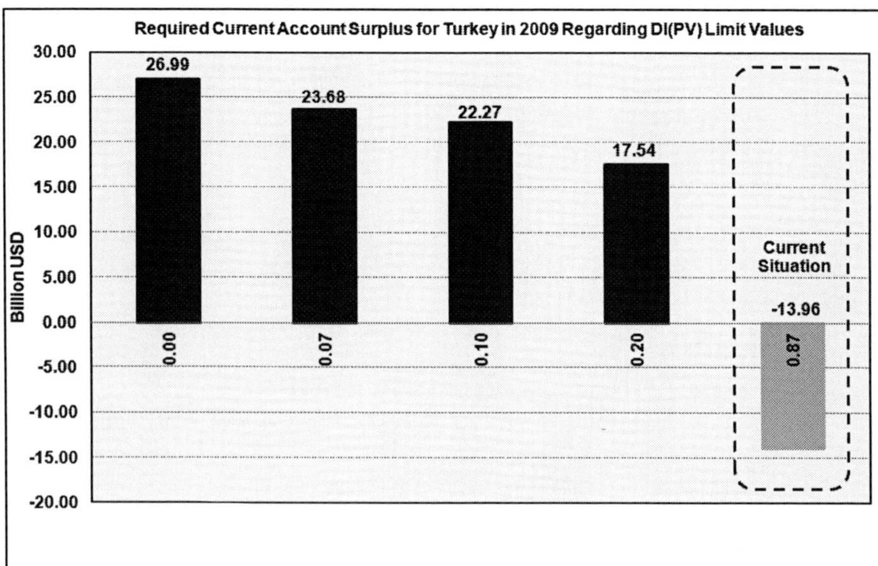

CHAPTER ELEVEN

CONCLUSION

As a result of this study, for an economic dependency level that allows Turkey to protect its own interests in terms of economic and political decisions and to act independently, the DI(PV)[1] value should be in the range of 0.00-0.07. In practical terms, this means that the relation determined between the variables of current account surplus (deficit) and External Debt, which make up the DI(PV) value, should be protected. The relation stated as the result of the study is given by formula number 3:

DI(PV) = (-9.8821xCurrent Deficit/GNP)+ (0.9945xExternal Debt /GNP)

In an economy with a current account deficit where, out of the variables used in the formula, current account deficit has a negative sign and External Debt has a positive sign, and with the presence of External Debt, it cannot be possible to reach the above mentioned DI(PV) values. Therefore, current account deficit can form only at the limit DI(PV) value (0.07) and in a 0 External Debt situation, Current Deficit/GDP ratio however, should be at a very low level like -0.71%. In a situation where the DI(PV) is 0, which is the ideal situation, a Current Deficit possibility is mathematically not possible. All these results draw the attention to two main elements to reach the desired DI(PV) values:

Having a Current Account Surplus;
External Debt being at a Level that can be paid for by Current Account Surplus.

---

[1] In this study, Dependency Index was determined in two ways, as functions dependent on factors and variables, the DIN function was determined to be dependent on factors, and the DIN(PV) function was determined to be dependent on variables.

By taking the above mentioned points into account, the necessary current account surplus amounts calculated over Turkey's External Debt at the end of 2009 and the DI(PV)'s limit values are presented in Figure 10-3. By taking the determined limit values into account, External Debt level should be at a level that can be paid by current account surplus in 10-12 years.

The fact that results of the study are based on two main variables indirectly coincides with the main elements of the economic policies applied in the Ataturk period. The economic policy implemented by Ataturk is based on three main elements (Sabir, 2006, Aysan, 1980, p. 49, 89):

A strong domestic state treasury, a financial policy whose incomes are equal to expenses (Balanced Budget);
Balanced TL, which prevents inflation; a well-functioning banking system, a monetary policy whose resources and expenses are equal to each other;
A foreign economic relations policy which protects the power of the State Treasury in foreign economic relations and TL's value against foreign currencies, and aims to increase this value, and whose foreign currency revenues are equal to foreign currency expenses (Balance of Trade or Foreign Trade Surplus).

On the budget side, because of the belief that foreign borrowing and depreciation in the value of the currency are the results of budget deficits, in the economic policies of Ataturk, budget balance or surplus was a principle that should be protected relentlessly (Aysan, 1980, p. 31). Additionally, in this period, it was noted that state resources should be allocated for internal affairs, justice, national defence, foreign relations and national education, defined as the priority tasks of the state, general and supplementary budget revenues were allocated for these fundamental functions, while the remaining resources and borrowings were used for large scale investments, and it was opposed to borrowing for current spending. As a result, borrowings were not made for current spending in the general budget but they were made for investments that would create sources.

With the model in this study, it has been determined that there should be a current account surplus, External Debts should not be in the form of financing general budget deficits, but should be made for investments that have resource-creating potential, and should be at a level which can be paid by the current account surplus rate determined in the study.

In this way, while balanced and planned development is achieved, the target should be a decreased external dependency, and an economic structure should be established that will allow the protection of self-interests, not only from an economic, but also from a political point of view and enable Turkey to give itself room to act independently.

Following 1947, having abandoned this structure and transitioned to a free market economy, with the sources provided from outside in the first years, unplanned growth was attained, but Turkey started to experience current account deficit and payment crises due to this unplanned growth, and it had an economic structure dependent on the sources that would come from outside after the economic crisis in 1958. Turkey, while growth led to a current account deficit and internal and external sources were needed to finance this, did not have an economic structure to protect its self-interests, not only from an economic perspective, but also from the point of view of political decisions, nor did it have the ability to act independently.

Ataturk's opening speech of the Izmir Economics Congress on the 22nd of February 1923 (Sabir, 2006, Aysan, 1980, p. 21, Celebi, 2002):

> There is no civilised state which does not consider its economy before its army and navy. Full independence surely means independence in all areas like politics, finance, economics, justice, military and culture and full freedom. Deprivation from independence in any of the ones I cited means a real deprivation of a nation and country from its complete independence. The objective of our wars at present is full independence. And completion of independence is only possible with financial independence.

Ataturk's opening speech on the 1st of November 1937 (THS, 1961, p. 395): *The main principle that we follow in foreign trade is to protect the active character of our trade balance; because, it constitutes the most important principle in Turkish balance of payment."*

John Adams, US Vice President (1735-1826): *"There are two ways to conquer and enslave a nation. One is by the sword. The other is by debt."*

Figure 11-1 Ataturk, Getting Information Regarding Development in Domestic Industry in Domestic Goods Fair on 10 November 1934

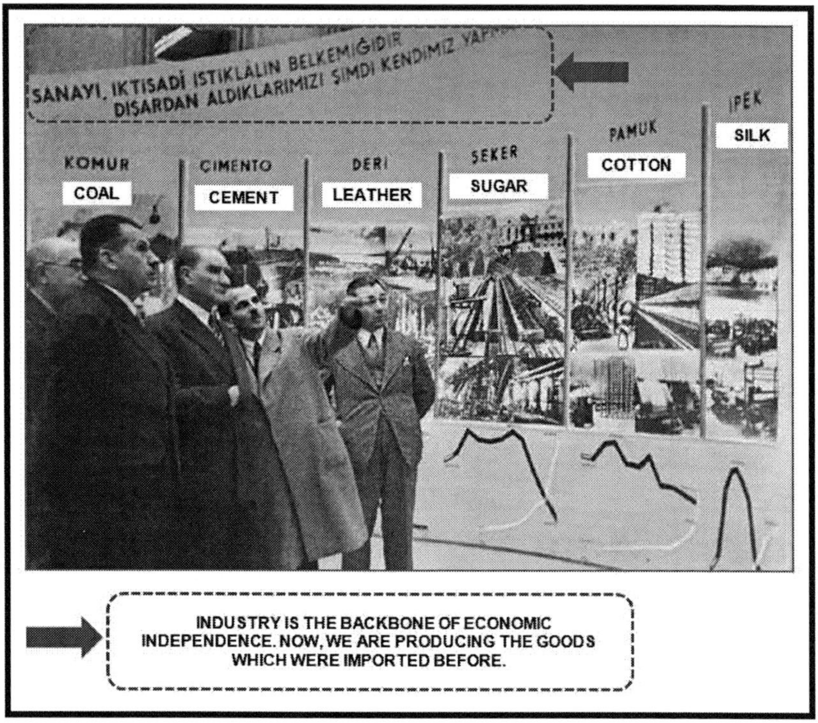

LIST OF ABBREVIATIONS

CBTR	Central Bank of Turkish Republic
DC	Developing Countries
DI	Dependency Index
DM	Deutsche Mark
DP	Democratic Party
ECLA	Economic Commission for Latin America
FX Rate	Foreign Exchange Rate
FYDP	Five Year Development Plan
GATT	General Agreement on Trade and Tariffs
GDC	Government Debt Securities
GDP	Gross Domestic Product
GNP	Gross National Product
IMF	International Monetary Fund
JP	Justice Party
kWh	Kilowatt hour (Electricity Consumption Unit)
M2	Time Deposits at Commercial Banks+M1 (Cash+Drawing Accounts at Commercial Banks+Central Bank Deposits)
NATO	North Atlantic Treaty Organisation
PEE	Public Economic Enterprise
PSBR	Public Sector Borrowing Requirement
PV	Powerful Variable
RPP	Republican People's Party
SCT	Special Consumption Tax
SEE	State Economic Enterprise
SOE	State Owned Enterprise
SPO	State Planning Organisation
SSI	State Statistical Institute
T-Bills	Treasury Bills
TETC	Turkish Electricity Transmission Corporation
THC	Turkish Historical Society
TL	Turkish Lira
TurkStat	Turkish Statistical Institute
UFT	Undersecretariat of Foreign Trade
USA	United States of America

USD	US Dollar
USSR	Union of Soviet Socialist Republics
UT	Undersecretariat of Treasury
VAT	Value Added Tax
WTO	World Trade Organisation

APPENDIX A

VARIABLE NO	DETAIL	1980	1981	1982	1983	1984	1985	1986	1987	1988	1989	1990	1991
1	Real GDP Growth (%)	-5.3	18.9	5.2	-3.3	5.7	10.6	11.4	-5.7	-1.3	4.2	7.8	-6.3
2	Change in Real FX Rate (%)	14.4	13.9	16.6	1.7	8.8	-2.3	-1.4	-17.4	-6.6	-11.1	-24.2	-6.6
3	Foreign Trade Deficit/ GDP (%)	-7.4	-6.0	-4.9	-5.8	-6.2	-5.1	-4.9	-4.6	-3.0	-3.9	-6.2	-4.9
4	Current Account Deficit/ GDP (%)	-5.1	-2.7	-1.5	-3.2	-2.5	-1.5	-2.0	-0.9	1.8	0.9	-1.7	0.2
5	Oil Imports /Current Account Deficit (%)	-0.87	-1.68	-3.70	-1.69	-2.34	-3.28	-1.23	-3.36	1.53	2.62	-1.33	9.82
6	Electricity Consumption/GDP (kWh/2008 USD)	0.13	0.15	0.19	0.21	0.26	0.26	0.26	0.26	0.28	0.27	0.22	0.24
7	Oil Prices (2008 USD/Barrel)	97.87	84.73	71.07	62.90	59.62	53.91	28.38	33.65	27.09	31.85	38.23	31.95
8	Export Coverage Ratios of Imports (%)	36.8	52.6	65.0	62.0	66.3	70.2	67.1	72.0	81.4	73.6	58.1	64.6
9	Capacity Utilization Rate of Manufacturing Industry(%)	55.2	56.7	59.4	60.3	74.3	70.3	70.0	78.2	74.8	72.8	75.2	74.0

VARIABLE NO	DETAIL	1980	1981	1982	1983	1984	1985	1986	1987	1988	1989	1990	1991
10	Direct Tax / Total Tax (%)	37.2	35.5	36.6	40.6	41.7	52.3	48.0	50.4	50.4	46.6	47.9	47.7
11	Total Budget Revenues/ Total Budget Expenses (%)	84.5	91.9	90.2	88.1	74.1	85.4	83.6	80.1	82.0	80.7	80.6	74.3
12	Total Debt / GDP (%)	37.1	36.2	40.9	54.0	56.6	58.5	63.5	70.1	67.0	59.8	49.3	50.9
13	PSBR (Public Sector Borrowing Requirement)/GDP (%)	8.9	4.0	3.6	4.9	5.4	3.6	3.7	6.1	4.8	5.4	7.4	10.2
14	M2/GDP (%)	16.9	20.7	24.3	23.6	23.5	23.2	23.8	23.6	21.0	20.7	18.2	18.6
15	Domestic Loan/GDP (%)	25.4	26.1	25.4	24.6	19.2	20.3	25.8	27.9	23.2	19.7	18.8	20.8
16	Budget Deficit/ GDP (%)	-3.2	-1.6	-1.5	-2.2	-4.5	-2.2	-2.8	-3.5	-3.0	-3.3	-3.4	-5.3
17	Foreign Currency Reserves/ Import (%)	16.5	10.4	12.2	13.6	11.5	9.0	12.3	12.1	16.1	30.6	26.8	23.4
18	External Debt/ Foreign Currency Reserves (%)	12.1	17.9	16.5	15.0	16.8	25.2	23.5	23.5	17.6	9.1	8.8	10.9

VARIABLE NO	DETAIL	1980	1981	1982	1983	1984	1985	1986	1987	1988	1989	1990	1991
19	Industrial Production Index (1997=100)	31.96	34.52	37.32	40.42	44.89	47.56	53.16	58.79	59.70	61.88	67.76	69.57
20	Private Sector Debt / GDP (%)	2.0	1.7	1.4	2.8	4.8	6.0	7.4	7.4	6.8	6.3	7.1	7.4
21	Unemployment Rate (%)	7.9	6.9	6.9	7.6	7.5	7.0	7.8	8.3	8.4	8.7	7.4	8.5
22	Real Domestic Debt Interest (% TL)	-46.8	-17.5	-18.5	-24.5	-30.2	-27.7	-17.8	-29.6	-35.0	-32.1	-25.6	-28.8
23	Short Term Capital Movement/GDP (%)	3.6	2.0	2.0	2.5	1.6	2.1	2.2	1.6	-1.9	-0.1	2.2	-2.1
24	External Debt Principal Payment+Import/ (Export+Foreign Currency Reserves) (%)	2.3	1.8	1.5	1.6	1.5	1.5	1.5	1.4	1.4	1.3	1.4	1.4
25	Short Term Capital Movement / Foreign Currency Reserves (%)	1.9	1.5	1.2	1.2	0.7	1.4	1.2	0.8	-0.8	0.0	0.6	-0.6
26	Treasury Bills USD Yield (%)	-53.5	-27.6	-30.1	-25.7	-35.8	-26.0	-16.6	-14.9	-30.4	-23.6	-1.9	-23.8

VARIABLE NO	DETAIL	1980	1981	1982	1983	1984	1985	1986	1987	1988	1989	1990	1991
27	Loss and Thief Ratio in Electricity (%)	12.2	11.7	12.3	12.3	11.9	12.8	14.5	13.3	13.7	12.7	12.3	13.2
28	External Debt/GDP (%)	23.3	23.6	28.1	31.2	35.5	38.6	42.9	47.1	45.0	41.3	34.7	35.5
29	Intermediate Goods Import/GDP (%)												

APPENDIX B

VARIABLE NO	DETAIL	1992	1993	1994	1995	1996	1997	1998	1999	2000	2001	2002	2003
1	Real GDP Growth (%)	4.5	6.0	-13.4	12.2	5.8	-2.0	6.7	-12.2	15.8	-15.0	20.0	9.5
2	Change in Real FX Rate (%)	-0.7	-6.6	20.0	-14.0	1.1	-5.9	0.1	-4.3	6.1	17.8	-6.4	-16.9
3	Foreign Trade Deficit /GDP (%)	-5.1	-7.8	-4.0	-8.3	-11.5	-12.0	-9.6	-7.8	-13.5	-7.0	-8.5	-9.2
4	Current Account Deficit/GDP (%)	-0.6	-3.6	2.0	-1.4	-1.4	-1.4	1.0	-0.5	-5.0	2.6	-0.3	-3.1
5	Oil Imports/ Current Account Deficit (%)	-2.70	-0.40	0.92	-1.25	-1.40	-1.21	1.04	-2.98	-0.42	1.03	-6.53	-0.64
6	Electricity Consumption /GDP (kWh/2008 USD)	0.26	0.26	0.39	0.34	0.37	0.40	0.42	0.48	0.49	0.70	0.58	0.48
7	Oil Prices (2008 USD/Barrel)	29.55	24.97	22.75	23.67	28.09	25.01	15.73	21.41	34.25	27.97	27.31	32.41
8	Export Coverage Ratios of Imports (%)	64.3	52.1	77.8	60.6	53.2	54.1	58.7	65.4	51.0	75.7	69.9	68.1
9	Capacity Utilization Rate of Manufacturing Industry (%)	76.4	79.6	72.9	78.6	78.0	79.4	76.5	72.4	75.9	70.9	75.4	78.4

VARIABLE NO	DETAIL	1992	1993	1994	1995	1996	1997	1998	1999	2000	2001	2002	2003
10	Direct Tax/ Total Tax (%)	49.6	51.4	51.7	57.5	60.6	59.3	53.4	54.7	59.1	59.6	66.3	67.0
11	Total Budget Revenues/ Total Budget Expenses (%)	78.6	72.4	83.0	81.5	68.6	72.0	76.3	67.7	72.4	64.5	66.2	71.6
12	Total Debt/ GDP (%)	54.5	57.1	73.4	62.2	65.9	67.3	71.0	86.4	89.1	148.0	124.7	113.8
13	PSBR (Public Sector Borrowing Requirement)/GDP (%)	10.6	10.3	6.2	5.0	8.8	7.8	9.6	15.7	11.9	16.3	12.6	9.3
14	M2/GDP (%)	17.4	14.3	16.3	16.2	19.8	19.6	21.9	29.2	26.3	26.3	22.0	22.5
15	Domestic Loan/GDP (%)	22.4	22.9	20.0	20.9	24.8	27.5	22.5	22.4	23.0	20.2	13.2	15.0
16	Budget Deficit / GDP (%)	-4.3	-6.8	-3.9	-4.1	-8.4	-7.8	-7.1	-11.7	-10.3	-16.0	-14.1	-11.1
17	Foreign Currency Reserves/ Import (%)	26.7	21.1	30.6	34.7	37.3	37.9	42.9	57.0	40.7	45.4	52.0	48.5
18	External Debt /Foreign Currency Reserves (%)	9.6	11.3	9.7	6.1	4.9	4.6	4.9	4.4	5.3	6.0	4.8	4.3

VARIABLE NO	DETAIL	1992	1993	1994	1995	1996	1997	1998	1999	2000	2001	2002	2003
19	Industrial Production Index (1997=100)	73.00	78.90	74.04	83.45	89.70	100.09	101.30	97.54	103.43	94.45	103.40	112.44
20	Private Sector Debt / GDP (%)	9.7	13.1	13.2	12.8	15.0	18.1	21.3	26.5	27.5	29.5	23.5	20.3
21	Unemployment Rate (%)	8.4	9.2	8.3	7.3	6.3	7.2	6.7	7.4	9.3	12.4	14.5	13.8
22	Real Domestic Debt Interest (% TL)	-25.8	-30.3	-37.8	-19.5	-11.6	-28.7	-4.0	-7.0	17.5	-12.6	3.6	10.3
23	Short Term Capital Movement/ GDP (%)	1.8	4.6	-3.4	2.4	2.7	3.4	-0.8	2.9	6.5	-5.0	3.6	2.4
24	External Debt Principal Payment+ Import/ (Export+ Foreign Currency Reserves) (%)	1.7	2.1	1.9	1.7	1.9	1.7	1.6	1.4	1.8	1.7	1.5	1.4

VARIABLE NO	DETAIL	1992	1993	1994	1995	1996	1997	1998	1999	2000	2001	2002	2003
25	Short Term Capital Movement/ Foreign Currency Reserves (%)	0.5	1.3	-0.6	0.3	0.3	0.3	-0.1	0.2	0.6	-0.4	0.2	0.2
26	Treasury Bills USD Yield (%)	-25.2	-25.4	-48.1	-6.4	-12.6	-24.2	-4.1	-2.8	10.8	-25.8	10.7	32.7
27	Loss and Thief Ratio in Electricity (%)	14.2	14.6	16.0	16.8	17.5	18.4	19.1	19.1	19.4	19.3	18.8	17.6
28	External Debt/GDP (%)	36.8	39.0	52.7	44.7	44.6	45.5	48.7	56.8	59.9	79.5	70.7	59.8
29	Intermediate Goods Import/GDP (%)									18.2	21.2	20.6	20.6

APPENDIX C

VARIABLE NO	DETAIL	2004	2005	2006	2007	2008
1	Real GDP Growth (%)	9.4	5.1	7.9	2.6	2.4
2	Change in Real FX Rate (%)	-12.9	-12.5	-2.3	-16.8	-8.4
3	Foreign Trade Deficit/GDP (%)	-11.3	-11.9	-13.5	-12.7	-12.6
4	Current Account Deficit/GDP (%)	-4.8	-6.1	-8.0	-7.7	-7.6
5	Oil Imports/Current Account Deficit (%)	-0.42	-0.39	-0.33	-0.31	-0.37
6	Electricity Consumption/GDP (kWh/2008 USD)	0.42	0.39	0.40	0.36	0.34
7	Oil Prices (2008 USD/Barrel)	42.93	55.17	62.26	66.67	91.48
8	Export Coverage Ratios of Imports (%)	64.8	62.9	61.3	63.1	65.4
9	Capacity Utilization Rate of Manufacturing Industry (%)	81.3	80.3	81.0	81.8	78.1
10	Direct Tax/Total Tax (%)	68.9	69.4	68.5	66.1	64.9
11	Total Budget Revenues/Total Budget Expenses (%)	78.5	93.4	97.4	92.9	92.3
12	Total Debt/GDP (%)	105.3	96.9	95.3	90.2	88.4
13	PSBR (Public Sector Borrowing Requirement)/GDP (%)	4.7	-0.4	-2.6	0.1	1.1
14	M2/GDP (%)	25.4	31.4	32.1	34.9	39.0
15	Domestic Loan/GDP (%)	19.4	27.3	32.4	37.4	41.0
16	Budget Deficit/GDP (%)	-7.0	-2.0	-0.8	-2.3	-2.4

VARIABLE NO	DETAIL	2004	2005	2006	2007	2008
17	Foreign Currency Reserves/Import (%)	36.9	43.3	43.6	43.1	35.2
18	External Debt / Foreign Currency Reserves (%)	4.5	3.4	3.4	3.4	3.9
19	Industrial Production Index (1997=100)	123.47	130.07	137.68	145.08	141.80
20	Private Sector Debt /GDP (%)	21.1	23.1	30.0	32.3	33.6
21	Unemployment Rate (%)	10.8	10.6	10.2	10.3	11.0
22	Real Domestic Debt Interest (% TL)	13.5	8.4	5.6	7.7	6.3
23	Short Term Capital Movement/GDP (%)	4.0	7.8	4.7	5.0	3.5
24	External Debt Principal Payment+Import/(Export+ Foreign Currency Reserves) (%)	1.5	1.5	1.5	1.4	1.5
25	Short Term Capital Movement/Foreign Currency Reserves (%)	0.3	0.6	0.3	0.3	0.3
26	Treasury Bills USD Yield (%)	30.3	23.9	8.1	29.4	16.0
27	Loss and Thief Ratio in Electricity (%)	16.0	15.4	14.6	14.5	14.4
28	External Debt/GDP (%)	53.1	46.7	51.7	50.4	50.3
29	Intermediate Goods Import/GDP (%)	22.3	22.5	24.8	25.0	27.4

BIBLIOGRAPHY

Aysan, M.A. (1980). *On 100th Birth Year Ataturk's Economic Policy*. Istanbul: Economic and Social Publications.

Boratav, K. (2009). *Turkish Economic History 1908-2007*. Istanbul: Image Publishing House

Cavanagh, J. (2009). No Consensus on the Washington Consensus. Viewed on 10th of November 2009 and retrieved from: http://www.tni.org/archives/cavanagh_noconsensus

Celebi, E. (2002), Ataturk's Economic Reforms and Their Effects on Turkish Economy (1923-2002). *Journal of Dogus University* (5), p. 17-50.

Central Bank of Turkish Republic (CBTR) (2009a). Inflation Data, 2001-2008. Viewed on 22nd of September 2009 and retrieved from CBTR Electronic Data Distribution System Information Portal: http://evds.tcmgb.gov.tr/cbt.html.

—. (2009b). Revenues Received from Privatisations, 1986-2008. Viewed on 15th of November 2009 and retrieved from CBTR Electronic Data Distribution System Information Portal: http://evds.tcmgb.gov.tr/cbt.html

—. (2009c). Domestic Loan Volume, 1990-2008. Viewed on 15th of November 2009 and retrieved from CBTR Electronic Data Distribution System Information Portal: http://evds.tcmgb.gov.tr/cbt.html.

—. (2009d). USD FX Rate, 1990-2008. Viewed on 15th of November 2009 and retrieved from CBTR Electronic Data Distribution System Information Portal: http://evds.tcmgb.gov.tr/cbt.html

Cinko, L. (2008), an Assessment on Financial Crisis Theories. Marmara University Banking and Insurance Academy, International Finance Symposium, Global Fluctuations and their Reflections on Finance Sector, p. 325-334.

Cosar, N. (1996a). Financing Policies in Republican Era (1924-1938), Encyclopaedia of Money and Finance (1), p. 340-355, Istanbul: Creative Publishing House.

—. (1996b), Public Financing Policy in World War II Years, *Encyclopaedia of Money and Finance* (3), p. 801-814, Istanbul: Creative Publishing House.

—. (1996c), Payment of Ottoman Debts after Lausanne Agreement, *Encyclopaedia of Money and Finance* (3), p. 1175-1183, Istanbul: Creative Publishing House.

—. (1997, August), Financial Approaches After World War II, *Social History* (44), p. 48-57.

—. (2005, March), Finance Policy in Democratic Party Period, *Journal of Faculty of Political Sciences* (60-1), p. 29-58.

Ekzen, N. (2008). From 1980 Washington Consensus - 2007/08 Washington Crisis: Alternative is always IMF. Viewed on 18th of November 2009 and retrieved from: http://www.bagimsizsosyalbilimciler.org/Yazilar_Uye/EkzenDec08.pdf.

Eren A. and Suslu, B. (2001 September-October). In the Light of Financial Crisis Theories General Assessment of Crises Experienced in Turkey. *New Turkey* (41), p: 662-674.

Ertuna, I.O. (2007). *Turkish Economy on the Verge of New Century.* Istanbul: ICCPA Publications.

Inan, A. (1972). *Etatism Principle and First Industry Plan of Turkish Republic 1933.* Ankara: Turkish Historical Society Printing House.

Isik, S., Duman, K. and Korkmaz, A. (2004). Financial Crises in Turkish Economy: A Factor Analysis Application. *D.E.U.F.E.A.S. Journal,* (19-1), p. 45-69.

Karacor, Z. and Alptekin, V. (2006). Assessment of Financial Crises Through Forecasting in Advance: Turkey Example. *Journal of Management and Economics,* (13-2), p. 237-256.

Kazgan, G. (2009). A Comparative Exploration on Crises in Turkish Economy (1929-2001) Their Causes and Consequences. Viewed on 15th of November 2009 and retrieved from Information Portal: http://kazgan.bilgi.edu.tr/docs/Turkiye.doc

Mangir, F. (2009). Effects of Financial Deregulation (1989–2001) on Turkish Economy: November 2000 and February 2001 Crises. Viewed on 30th of November 2009 and retrieved from Information Portal: http://www.sosyalbil.selcuk.edu.tr/sos_mak/makaleler/Fatih%20MANGIR/MANGIR,%20Fatih.pdf

Olken, B.A. and Jones, B. F. (2005, August). The Anatomy of Start-Stop Growth. *National Bureau of Economic Research* (Discussion Paper No. 11528).

Oyan, O. (1999, October), Changing Structure of Budgets, Education Union *Seminar Notes for Trainers and Managers*, p. 25-32.

Ozcelik, O. and Tuncer, G. (2007, Haziran). Ataturk Era Economic Policies. *Afyon Kocatepe University Journal of Social Sciences* (9-1), p. 253-266.

Ozdemir, B. (2009a). Role of Washington Consensus in Economic Development and Situation of Turkey Viewed on 22nd of February 2010 and retrieved from Information Portal: http://www.akademiktisat.net/calisma/gelisme_iktisat/kalkinma_washington_bozdemir.htm

—. (2009b). Ottoman State's External Debts. Ankara: ACC Publications.

Pakdemirli, E. (2003). *Economic Figures of Republican Era (1923-2002)*. Ankara: UCCE.

Pamuk, S. (2008). *Globalisation from Ottomans to Republic, Economic Policies and Growth*. Istanbul: Turkey Is Bank Culture Publications.

Rodrik, D. (2006, December). Goodbye Washington Consensus, Hello Washington Confusion. *Journal of Economic Literature* (44-4), s. 973-987.

Rozaliyev, Y.N. (1978). *Development Characteristics of Capitalism in Turkey (1923-1960)*. Ankara: Onur Publications.

Sabir, H. (July-September 2006). Ataturk's Economy Understanding. *Court of Accounts Journal* (62), p. 3-19.

Sak, G. and Caglar, E. (2009) From Washington Consensus to Istanbul Decisions: Where are we heading to? Viewed on 22nd of December 2009 and retrieved from Information Portal: http://yeni.tepav.org.tr/upload/files/1271313242r6794.Istanbul_Kararlari.pdf

Schmitz, H. (1996). *Industrialisation Strategies in Underdeveloped Countries: Lessons to be Drawn from Historical Experience, Rise and Fall of Development Economics*. Istanbul: Iletisim Publications.

Soyak, A. and Eroglu, N. (2008, March). Role of IMF-World Bank Structural Adjustment Policies in Transformation of Turkey's Development Perspective. *MPRA*. (MPRA Paper No: 11446).

SPO (2005). *Seventh Five-Year Development Plan (1996-2000)*. Ankara: SPO Printing House

State Statistical Institution (SSI-TSI) (2001). *Statistical Indicators 1923-1998*, Ankara: State Statistical Institution Printing House

Stiglitz, J.E., (2002). Globalisation Great Disappointment. Istanbul: Plan B Publications.

Tunc, T. (2001, Bahar). Industry Breakthroughs in Kemalist Era, *METU Ataturkist Ideas Society Thought Journal* (13), p. 48-52.

Turkish Historical Society (THS). (1961). *Ataturk's Speeches and Statements*. Ankara: Turkish Historical Society

Turkish Statistical Institution (TSI) (2008a). Gross national product (with current prices) by periods, 1987-2007. Viewed on 27th of March 2008 and retrieved from Information Portal: http://www.tuik.gov.tr/PreIstatistikTablo.do?istab_id=520

—. (2008b). Foreign Trade by Years, 1923–2006. Viewed on 27th of March 2008 and retrieved from Information Portal: http://www.tuik.gov.tr/PreTablo.do?tb_id=12&tb_adi=Dış%20Ticaret %20İstatistikleri&ust_id=4

Ugur, B. (2007). 1923-1940 Period and Effect of 1929 Depression. Viewed on 27th of March 2008 and retrieved from Information Portal: www.geocities.com/ceteris_paribus_tr/b_ugur.doc.

Undersecretariat of Foreign Trade (UFT) (2008a). World Exports (1995–2005). Viewed on 19th of January 2008 and retrieved from Information Portal: http://www.dtm.gov.tr/dtmadmin/upload/EAD/IstatistikDb/ihracat.pdf.

—. (2008b). World Imports (1995–2005). Viewed on 19th of January 2008 and retrieved from Information Portal: http://www.dtm.gov.tr/dtmadmin/upload/EAD/IstatistikDb/ithalat.pdf.

—. (2010a). World Exports (1998–2008). Viewed on 2nd of October 2010 and retrieved from Information Portal: http://www.dtm.gov.tr/dtmadmin/upload/EAD/KonjokturIzlemeDb/ihr acat.pdf.

—. (2010b). World Imports (1998–2008). Viewed on 2nd of October 2010 and retrieved from Information Portal:: http://www.dtm.gov.tr/dtmadmin/upload/EAD/KonjokturIzlemeDb/ith alat.pdf

Undersecretariat of Treasury (2008a). Monthly Economic Indicators, Public Finance. Viewed on 20th of March 2008 and retrieved from Information Portal: http://www.hazine.gov.tr/stat/egosterge/VI-KamuMaliyesi/Kamu%20 Maliyesi.xls

—. (2008b). Monthly Economic Indicators, Foreign Trade and Balance of Payments. Viewed on 20th of March 2008 and retrieved from Information Portal: http://www.hazine.gov.tr/stat/egosterge/V-DisTicaretveOdemeler Dengesi/Dis%20Ticaret%20ve%20Odemeler%20Dengesi.xls

—. (2008c). Turkey's Net External Debt Stock. Viewed on 20th of March 2008 and retrieved from Information Portal: http://www.hazine.gov.tr/stat/NET%20DIS%20BORC%20STOKU%2 0-%20NET%20EXTERNAL%20DEBT.xls#'NET DIS BORC STOK-NET EXT DEBT'!A1

—. (2008d). Domestic Borrowing Status By Years. Viewed on 20th of March 2008 and retrieved from Information Portal: http://www.hazine.gov.tr/stat/YILLIK_VERILER.xls#yillik_borc!A1

—. (2008e). Consolidated Budget Balance. Viewed on 20th of March 2008 and retrieved from Information Portal: http://www.hazine.gov.tr/yayin/hazineistatistikleri/2-1A.xls

—. (2008f). Turkey's Gross External Debt Stock. Viewed on 20th of March 2008 and retrieved from Information Portal: http://www.hazine.gov.tr/stat/BRUT%20DIS%20BORC%20STOK%20-%20GROSS%20EXTERNAL%20DEBT%20WEB.xls

Ural, M. (2003). Financial Crises and Turkey, *D.E.U F.E.A.S. Journal* (18-1), p. 11-28.

World Bank (2009). World GDP. Viewed on 15th of November 2009 and retrieved from Information Portal: http://ddp-ext.worldbank.org/ext/DDPQQ/member.do?method=getMembers&userid=1&queryId=135.

Yay, G.G. (2001, November-December). Financial Crises in 1990s and Turkey Crisis. *New Turkey Economic Crisis Special Edition II*, No: 42, p.1234-1248.

Yeldan, E. (2002,Yaz). Assessments on Development Discourse of Neoliberal Globalisation Ideology. *Praksis Journal (7)*, p. 19-34.

Yurdakul, F. (2001, March). Structural Breakdowns in Inflation Process in Turkey. *Journal of Faculty of Political Sciences* (56-1), p. 149-169.

INDEX